About BOOKSHELF ADVENTURES

This handbook is Unit V in a uniquely developed multidisciplinary series created with the elementary student, the teacher, the librarian, and the curriculum in mind. Called "Guided Research Discovery Units," the series includes six self-contained handbooks, each presenting a number of reproducible activity units related to a particular curriculum area:

Unit I   ANIMALS! ANIMALS! ANIMALS! *(Natural Science)*
Unit II   IT'S A SMALL WORLD! *(Geography)*
Unit III FASCINATING PEOPLE! *(History)*
Unit IV   FUN PAC! *(Language Arts)*
Unit V   BOOKSHELF ADVENTURES *(Children's Literature)*
Unit VI   BLAST OFF! *(Space Science)*

Through the completely organized, directed research projects in each handbook, students and teachers are introduced to universally appealing topics that can be explored by each individual at his or her own level of competency and speed. Each project focuses on finding certain facts, recording the facts, and rewriting the facts in sentence form. Every page of each project is designed differently to entice, captivate, or stimulate the students involved in research/reference work.

BOOKSHELF ADVENTURES includes five projects suggested for students ages 10-14. Each of them can be used effectively to:

- develop a unit of study
- supplement a unit of study
- develop language, research, and reading skills through an interesting topic that may be, but is not necessarily, curriculum-related
- assist the teacher or librarian in organizing his or her presentation to the class or individual students before actual use of the projects
- promote creativity instead of copying in reference/research work
- provide meaningful and challenging activities for the gifted or enthusiastic individual working beyond the classroom environment
- extend or culminate research skills already taught in the classroom or resource center
- motivate students who are "turned off" to working on research/reference projects

The all-inclusive "Teacher's Guide" enables you as a teacher or librarian to use these projects in a variety of ways so that they will prove to be a most valuable asset to your school program.

Nancy M. Hall
Ruth V. Snoddon

About the Authors

Ruth V. Snoddon, M.A., Northern Michigan University (Marquette), B.A., Laurentian University (Sudbury, Ontario), has been involved in elementary education for the past 24 years as a classroom teacher and as a librarian. She has worked with curriculum committees, presented workshops on professional development, and compiled a policy manual for school library resource centers.

Nancy M. Hall, B.A., Laurentian University, has taught for 14 years and has experience in the library and in the classroom. Recently, she developed a language arts course of study for her school. Mrs. Hall is presently working on her M.A. in elementary education at Northern Michigan University.

Table of Contents

Teacher's Guide: *Pages*

    Suggestions for Use   5
    Research and Language Skills   5
    Bibliography   6
    Displaying Students' Work   7
    How to Make a Simple Mobile   8
    Above and Beyond   10

Research Projects:

Title	*Key*	
BARREL OF FUN	V — B1-9	11
HISTORICAL FICTION	V — H1-10	21
MYSTERY STORIES	V — M1-12	32
POETRY	V — P1-8	45
SCIENCE FICTION	V — S1-10	54

Teacher's Guide

The student projects in this Guided Research Unit can be used in a variety of ways. They require little or no preparation time other than that needed to duplicate the project outline pages for students. The contents are all inclusive and self-explanatory.

In the following, you will find specific suggestions for using the projects with your students, a listing of some of the reference/research and language skills developed by these activities, and guidelines for teaching students correct bibliographic form. Also included are directions for displaying students' finished work and ideas for additional project-related activities.

Suggestions for Use

The projects in each Discovery Unit can be used by individual students, small groups, or an entire class. They can also be used by an entire class divided into three or four groups (one group doing Historical Fiction, another Poetry, etc.) or by several pupils working on one project, with each assigned to do part and the completed work displayed as a cooperative effort.

Teachers and librarians can use the projects in many different ways, for example, as:

- a method for covering a particular subject area using the project as a guide for organizing a specific topic
- a group project for some, while other students work on the same topic using other ideas
- an extension or culmination of reference skills being taught within the classroom or resource center
- an enrichment program for individual students or groups of students working beyond the classroom environment
- a guide to note-taking

For instance, younger students in grades 2 or 3 might take notes cooperatively with teacher assistance and then use the project pages to write their notes on. Their completed project can be mounted on backing, made into a mobile or booklet, or displayed as the teacher desires.

Research and Language Skills

The following is just a partial listing of the research and language skills that are developed in these projects:

1. Following of printed directions
2. Focusing on a narrow topic that can be covered, e.g., *SCIENCE FICTION—AUTHOR—RAY BRADBURY*

3. Knowledge of some parts of books, e.g., title page and table of contents, and use of the index
4. Use of the card catalog (Author, Title, and Subject cards) and library organization (Dewey Decimal System and physical arrangement)
5. Searching out and locating relevant data from a wide variety of sources, i.e., encyclopedias, books, pictures, filmstrips, pamphlets, tapes, etc.
6. Selecting the most appropriate sources from materials gathered
7. Noting sources of information (Bibliography), i.e., Encyclopedia, Title(s), Volume No., Page No., Call No., and Other Sources. (*Note:* See the following section for a more extensive bibliographic form to use with the projects.)
8. Skimming for specific information from all sources used, with the focus on main ideas and key words
9. Writing the specific information collected in *note form* under appropriate headings on the outline provided (categorizing and summarizing)
10. Using gathered information from the outline and rewriting it in proper *sentence* and *paragraph* structure with emphasis on correct grammar and spelling

Bibliography

Beginning in the third or fourth grade, the young researcher should be taught and encouraged to use correct bibliographic form. There are three main pieces of information in a bibliography: the person (author, editor, performer), the title, and information regarding publication (city, publisher, and the copyright or publication date). The three sections are separated by periods. Titles of selections from an encyclopedia or a magazine appear within quotation marks. The second line of an entry is always indented. The items are arranged in alphabetical order and are numbered.

The teacher may use some discretion in abbreviating or adapting the format to local style. Bibliographic forms and examples follow.

Books

Author. *Title*. City of publication: Publisher, Copyright.

Examples:

1. Knight, Clayton. *Big Book of Helicopters*. New York: Grosset & Dunlap, Inc., 1971.
2. Sikorsky, Igor. *Story of the Winged-S*. New York: Dodd, Mead & Co., 1967.
3. Taylor, Michael J., & Taylor, John W. *Helicopters of the World*. New York: Charles Scribner's Sons, 1979.

Encyclopedia Articles

"Article." *Encyclopedia name*, Last copyright, Volume number, Page(s).

Example:

1. "Helicopter." *Encyclopedia Britannica*, 1972, 11, 314-316.

Teacher's Guide 7

Magazine and Newspaper Articles

Author (if known). "Article." *Magazine*, Volume number (Date), Page(s).

Example:

1. Weaver, Kenneth F. "The Incredible Universe." *National Geographic*, 145 (May 1974), 589.

Records, Tapes, Filmstrips

Title of Strip. (Filmstrip). Producer, Copyright (if available).

Example:

1. *War for Independence Bunker Hill* (Filmstrip). Encyclopedia Britannica Films, Inc., 1962.

Displaying Students' Work

Each guided research project in this unit has been developed so that students' work can be displayed in several forms. Suggestions for the most appropriate form of display are included with the particular project. Teachers, librarians, and students can also adapt other forms if they so desire.

The completed project can be:

- Mounted on a 24″ × 18″ piece of backing and displayed on a classroom bulletin board or elsewhere

- Made into a booklet

- Displayed as a mobile, as described in the next section

How to Make a Simple Mobile

Here are the materials and step-by-step directions for constructing a simple mobile with the project outlines.

You will need:

        2 sturdy plastic drinking straws
        lightweight yarn or string
        backing (construction paper or light bristol board)
        scissors
        glue
        paper puncher

Follow these steps to construct the mobile:

1. Glue the project shapes to the backing.

2. When the glue dries, cut out the shapes.

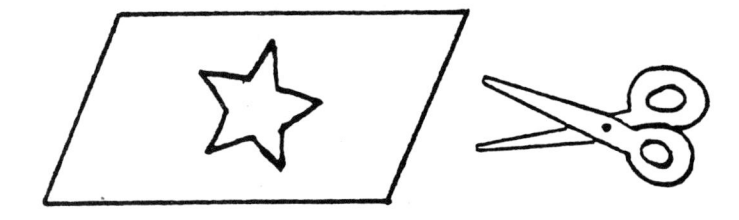

3. Punch a hole at the suitable location on each outline.

Teacher's Guide 9

4. Attach a string of varied length (from 24″ to 30″) to each shape and make a large knot at the end of each piece of string.

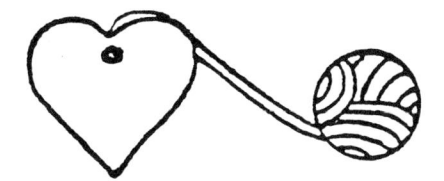

5. *Firmly* bind the straws together with yarn or string in the form of a cross.

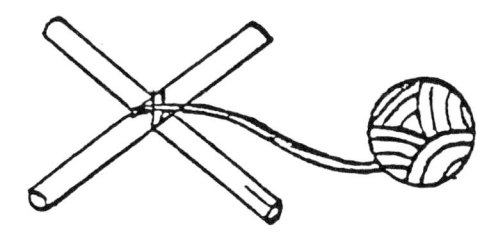

6. Cut a 1″ slit in the end of each straw and fasten each string by sliding the yarn through the slit below the knot (or just tie the string on firmly).
7. Tie string at the center of the crosspieces to suspend the mobile from the ceiling. Adjust the straws to balance the mobile evenly.
8. If desired, add the project title in whatever way desired.

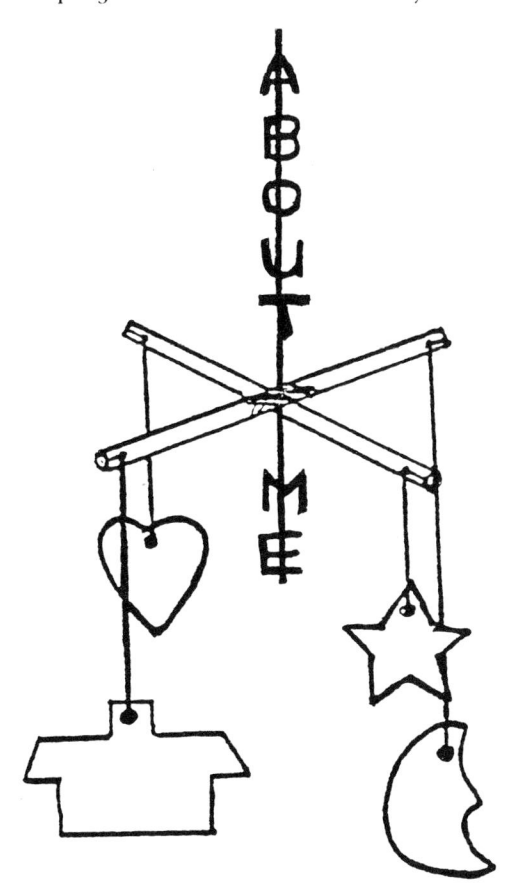

Above and Beyond

For the creative teacher and librarian, here are suggestions for other project-related activities.

Art Activities

pipe cleaner figures	sculptures
murals	TV programs
dioramas	collages
modeling	roll movies
puppets	picture painting
filmstrips	papier-mâché
soap carvings	

Language Arts Activities

1. Write a newscast or become a reporter or interviewer for your class.
2. Write a story or a poem to go with your topic.
3. Read a fiction story related to your topic and write a book report, diary or journal entry about it.
4. Learn how to spell and pronounce new words found in research materials you are using.
5. Use dictionary skills by making a glossary of important and unusual words related to your topic.
6. Collect newspaper or magazine articles, or pictures about your topic. Make these into a scrapbook or report to the class about the articles or pictures.
7. Display all print and nonprint materials in your class or school for others to view, i.e., articles from home or other completed activities such as those previously listed.

V — B

BARREL OF FUN

BARREL OF FUN V — B1

1. Check the sources you could use for this topic, for example: riddle books, joke books, poetry books, books containing facts, encyclopedias, and so on. Magazines and newspapers might also be useful. Choose as many sources as you need and list them on Bibliography page V — B2, using the form your teacher suggests.

2. Study the project papers. From your sources write all the necessary facts in NOTE FORM on the outline chart V — B3.

3. When all of your information has been gathered, rewrite it on the papers provided. This time use SENTENCES when possible. Proofread for spelling or grammar errors. Use markers, crayons, or colored pencils to color and outline the pictures.

4. Design your own title page for this unit and include: Title, Name of Editor (Your Name), Place of Publication (Name of Your School), and Year.

5. If you are a good worker, try the additional page called SUPER EFFORT. Add this to your finished project.

6. Write your own Table of Contents and Index Page.

7. Cut out the designs when completed and mount them on construction paper, make into a booklet, or use your own ideas for presentation to the class or individuals.

8. Your teacher will be glad to help you if you need any assistance.

9. APPROXIMATE TIME TO COMPLETE PROJECT: 6 — 8 hours.

BIBLIOGRAPHY

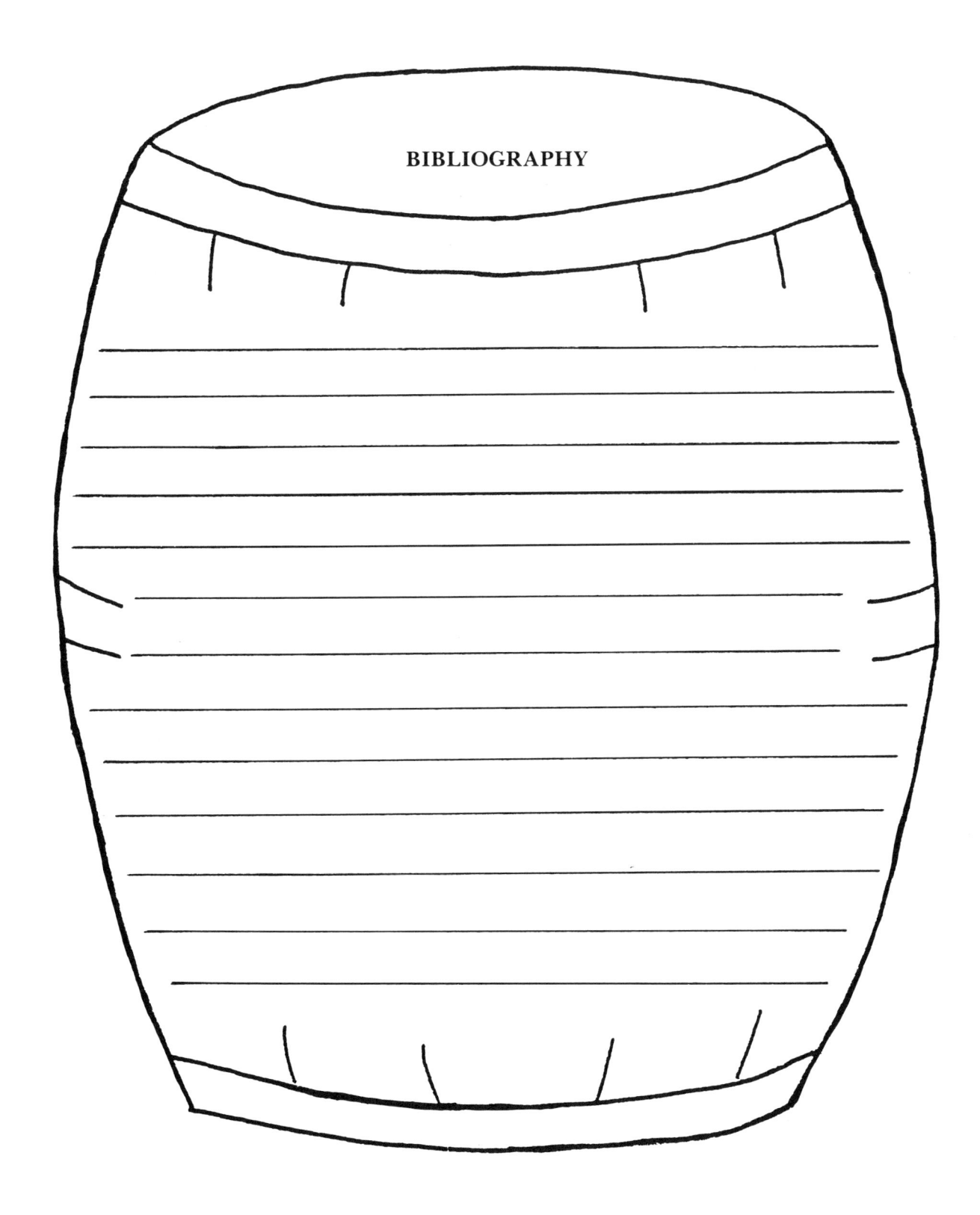

BARREL OF FUN   V — B3

Name_____

Date_____

JOKES AND RIDDLES

WHAT IS A JOKE?	WHAT IS A RIDDLE?

POETRY

WHAT IS HUMOROUS POETRY?	WHAT IS SERIOUS POETRY?

FASCINATING FACTS

WHAT DOES A BOOK ON FACTS TELL YOU?

JOKES AND RIDDLES   V — B4

WHAT IS A JOKE?

My favorite joke

Write your favorite joke taken from one of the joke books you have read.

JOKES AND RIDDLES　　　　　　　　　　　　　　　　　　　　V — B5

WHAT IS A RIDDLE?

_____
_____
_____
_____

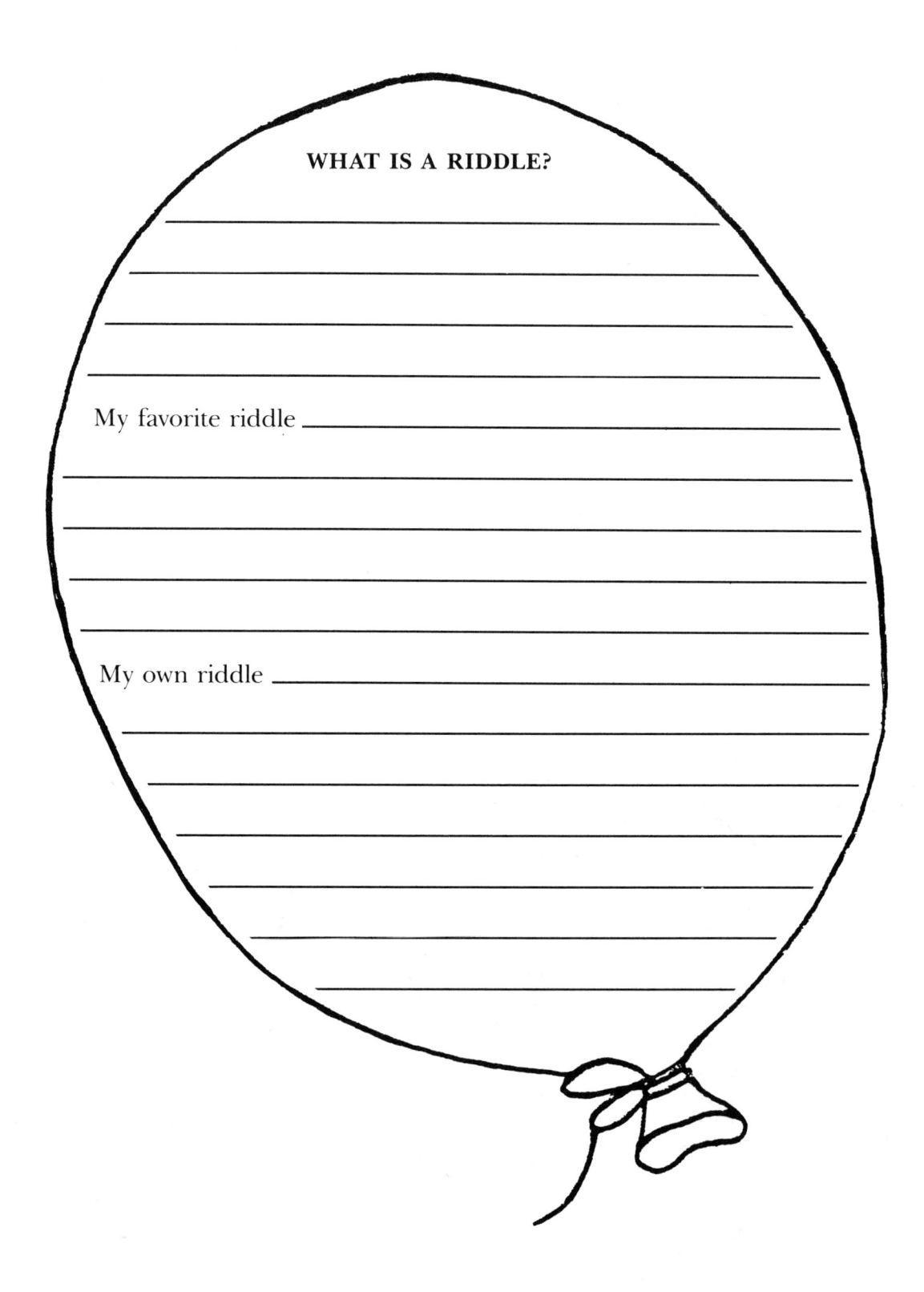

My favorite riddle _____
_____
_____
_____
_____

My own riddle _____
_____
_____
_____
_____
_____

Write your favorite riddle and include the answer. Then make up your own riddle and answer.

POETRY V — B6

WHAT IS HUMOROUS POETRY?

Write an example showing the kind of humorous poetry you like best, for example, a limerick.

POETRY V — B7

WHAT IS SERIOUS POETRY?

Copy a short serious poem (or part of a serious poem) from one of your poetry books to show that you know the difference between humorous and serious poetry.

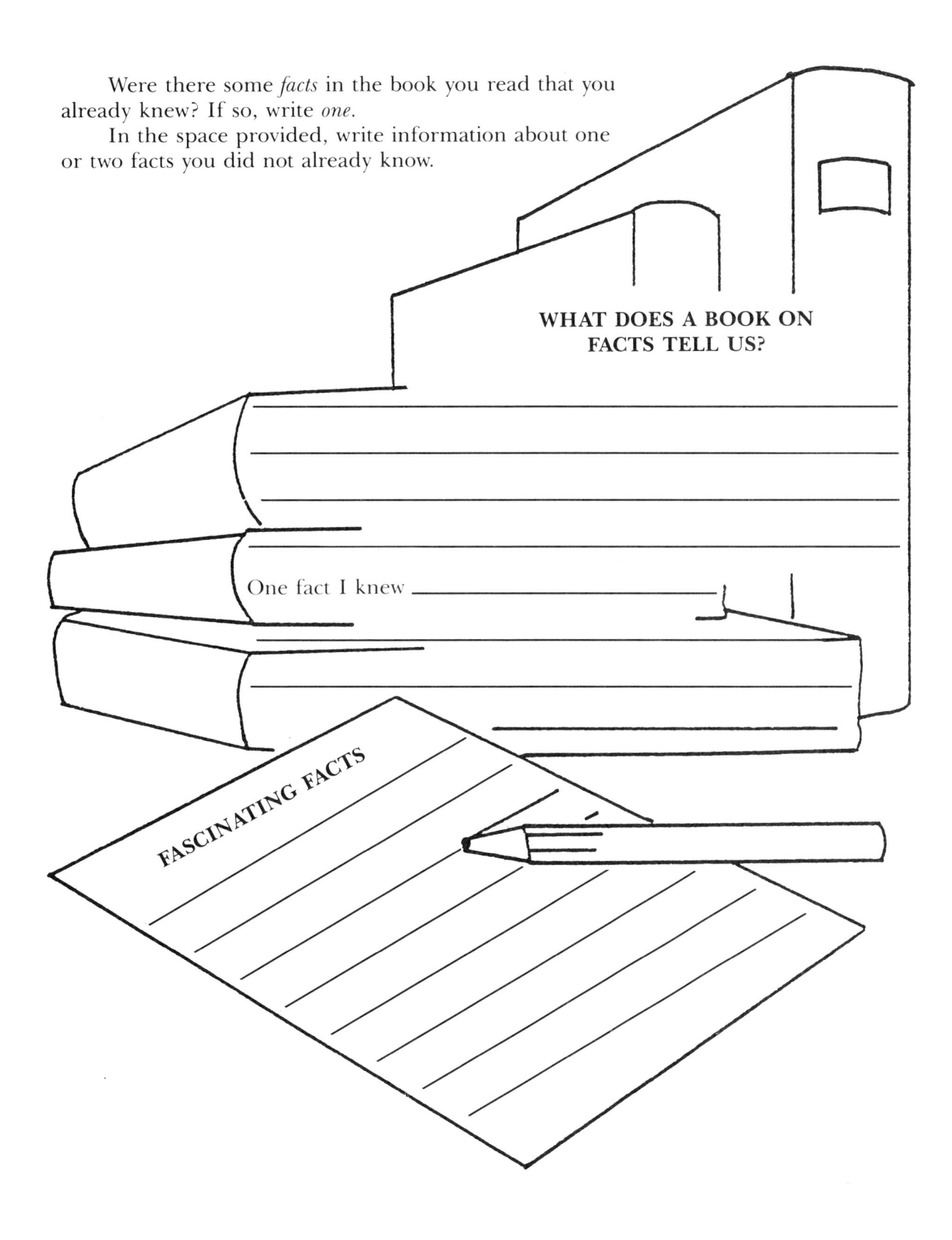

FASCINATING FACTS V — B8

Were there some *facts* in the book you read that you already knew? If so, write *one*.

In the space provided, write information about one or two facts you did not already know.

WHAT DOES A BOOK ON FACTS TELL US?

One fact I knew

FASCINATING FACTS

SUPER EFFORT   V — B9

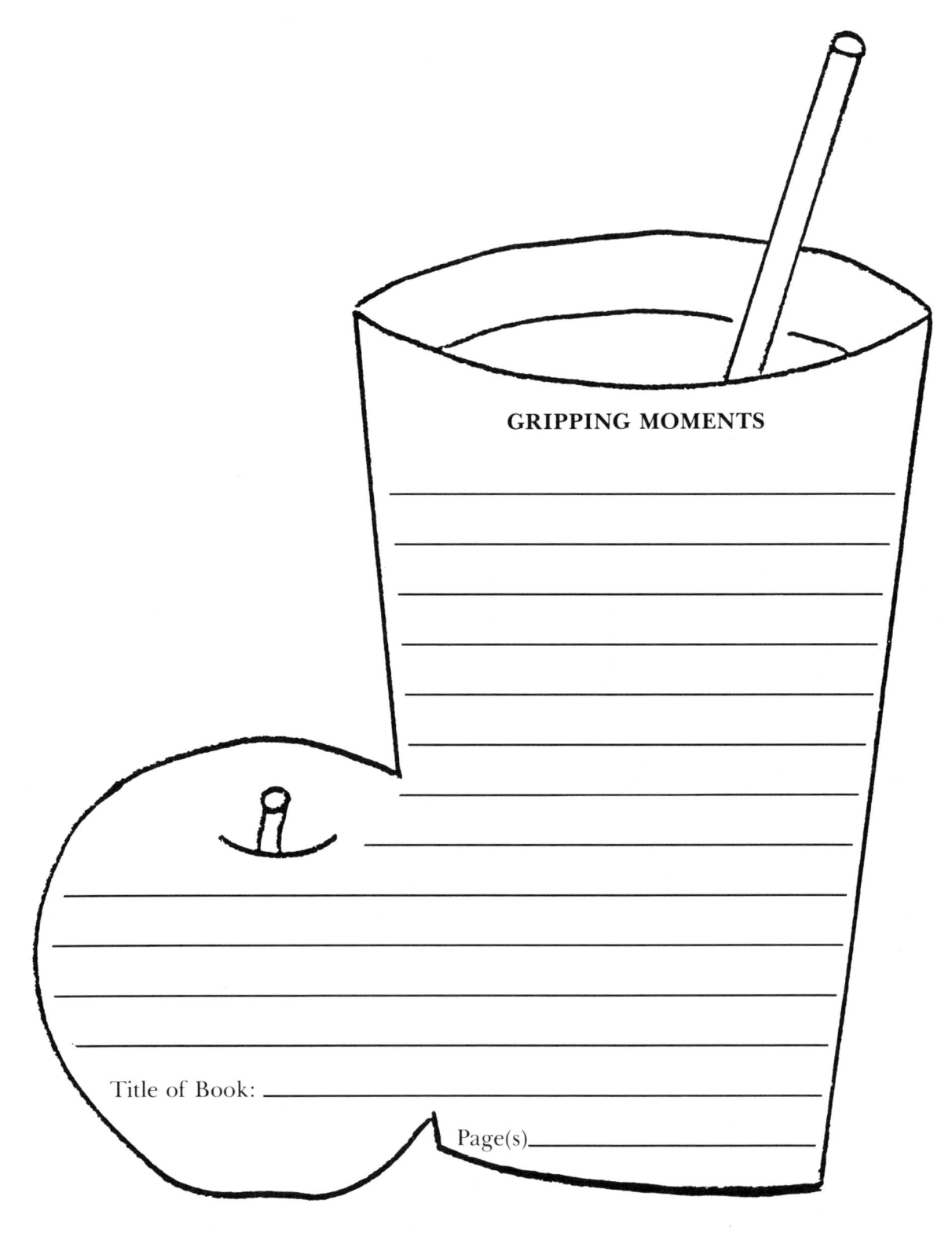

GRIPPING MOMENTS

_____
_____
_____
_____
_____
_____
_____
_____
_____
_____
_____

Title of Book: _____

Page(s) _____

Use a fiction or biography story you have read and choose a short exciting (suspenseful) selection from it to write about on this page. Name your source and page number(s).

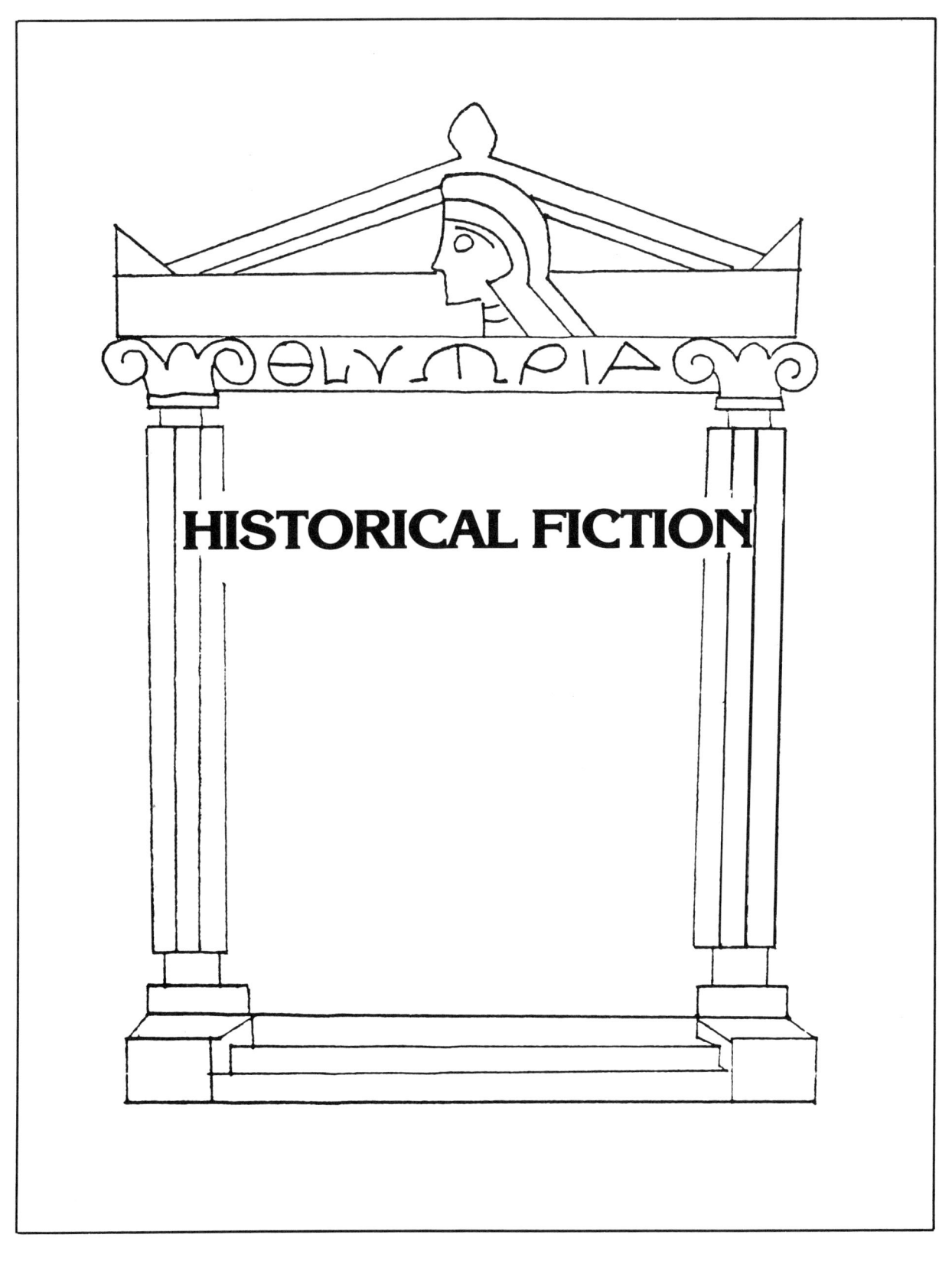

HISTORICAL FICTION

V—H

HISTORICAL FICTION   V — H1

1. Choose a historical fiction book to read. Suggestions may be offered by your teacher or librarian. I chose _____.

2. Use Bibliography page V — H2 to give the title of your book, the author's name, publisher, copyright date, and number of pages.

3. Study your project papers. After reading the book you have chosen, collect your information. Write the facts in NOTE FORM on outline chart V — H3.

4. When all of your information has been gathered, rewrite it on the papers provided. This time use SENTENCES. Proofread for spelling or grammar errors. Use markers, crayons, or colored pencils to color and outline the pictures.

5. If you are a good worker, try the additional page called SUPER EFFORT. Add this to your finished project.

6. Cut out the designs when completed and mount them on construction paper, make into a mobile, or use your own ideas for presentation to the class or individuals.

7. Your teacher will be glad to help you if you need any assistance.

8. APPROXIMATE TIME TO COMPLETE PROJECT: 4 — 5 hours. (This does not include the time you take to read your book.)

BIBLIOGRAPHY V — H2

BIBLIOGRAPHY

Title of book: _____

Author's name: _____

Publisher: _____

Copyright date: _____

Number of pages: _____

In the space provided, draw a small illustration to describe one part of your story.

HISTORICAL FICTION

V — H3

Name_____

I chose _____ Date_____

MAIN CHARACTERS: 1._____   2._____

3._____   (No more than 3)

DESCRIPTION OF MAIN CHARACTERS

PHYSICAL DESCRIPTION	**BEHAVIORAL DESCRIPTION**
1.	1.
2.	2.
3.	3.

MINOR CHARACTERS — NAME SEVERAL AND DESCRIBE BRIEFLY

TIME PERIOD IN HISTORY

WHEN DID THIS STORY TAKE PLACE?	**WHERE DID THIS STORY TAKE PLACE?**	**INTERESTING FACTS**

HOW DID THE EVENTS IN THE STORY AFFECT THE CHARACTERS INVOLVED?	**DO THE EVENTS OF THE STORY AFFECT US TODAY? HOW? WHY?**

DESCRIPTION OF MAIN CHARACTERS V — H4

MAIN CHARACTERS' PHYSICAL DESCRIPTIONS

1. Name: _____

_____
_____
_____
_____
_____
_____
_____

2. Name: _____

_____
_____
_____
_____
_____
_____

3. Name: _____

_____
_____
_____

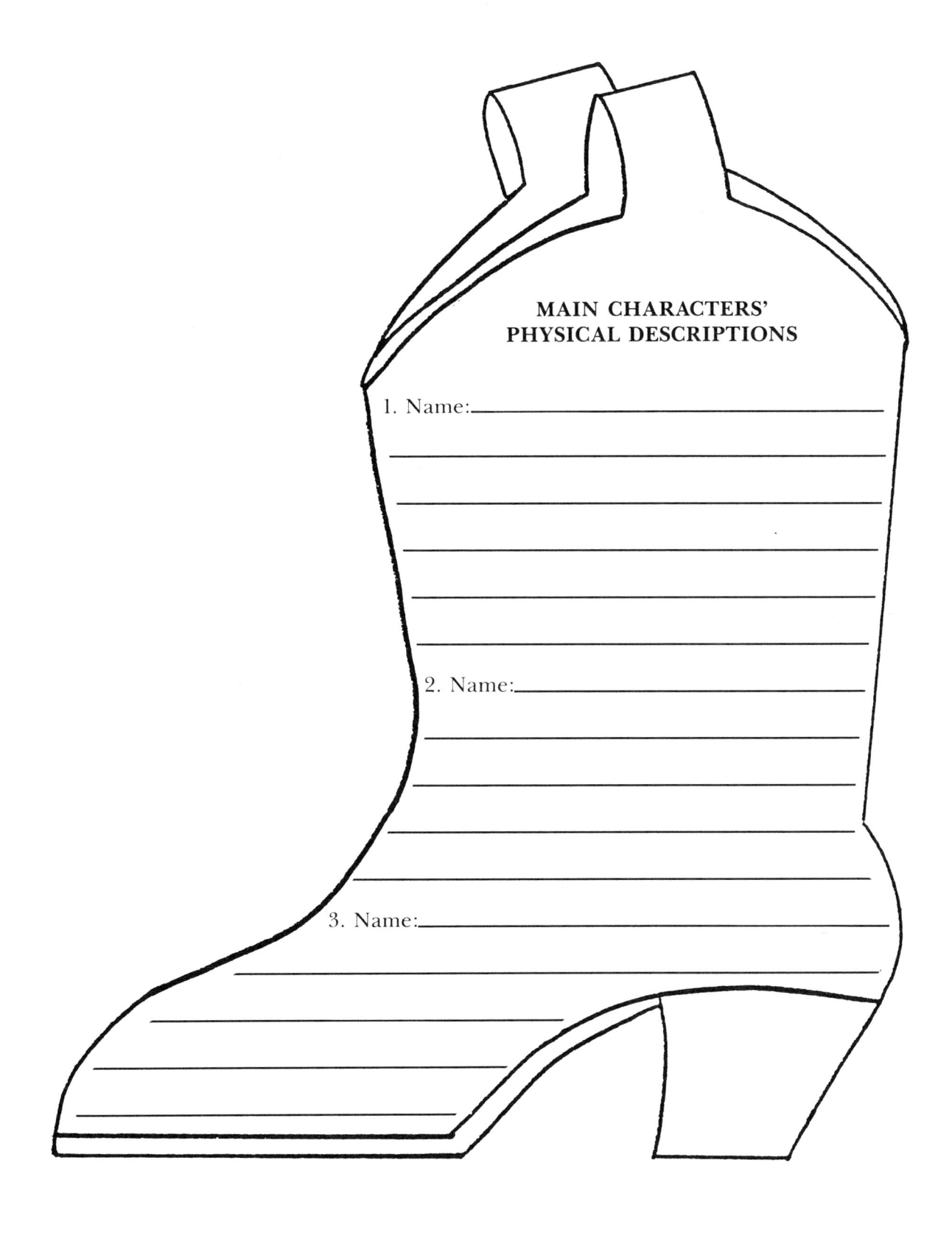

Did you tell your characters' ages and how they looked and dressed in the story you read?

DESCRIPTION OF MAIN CHARACTERS V — H5

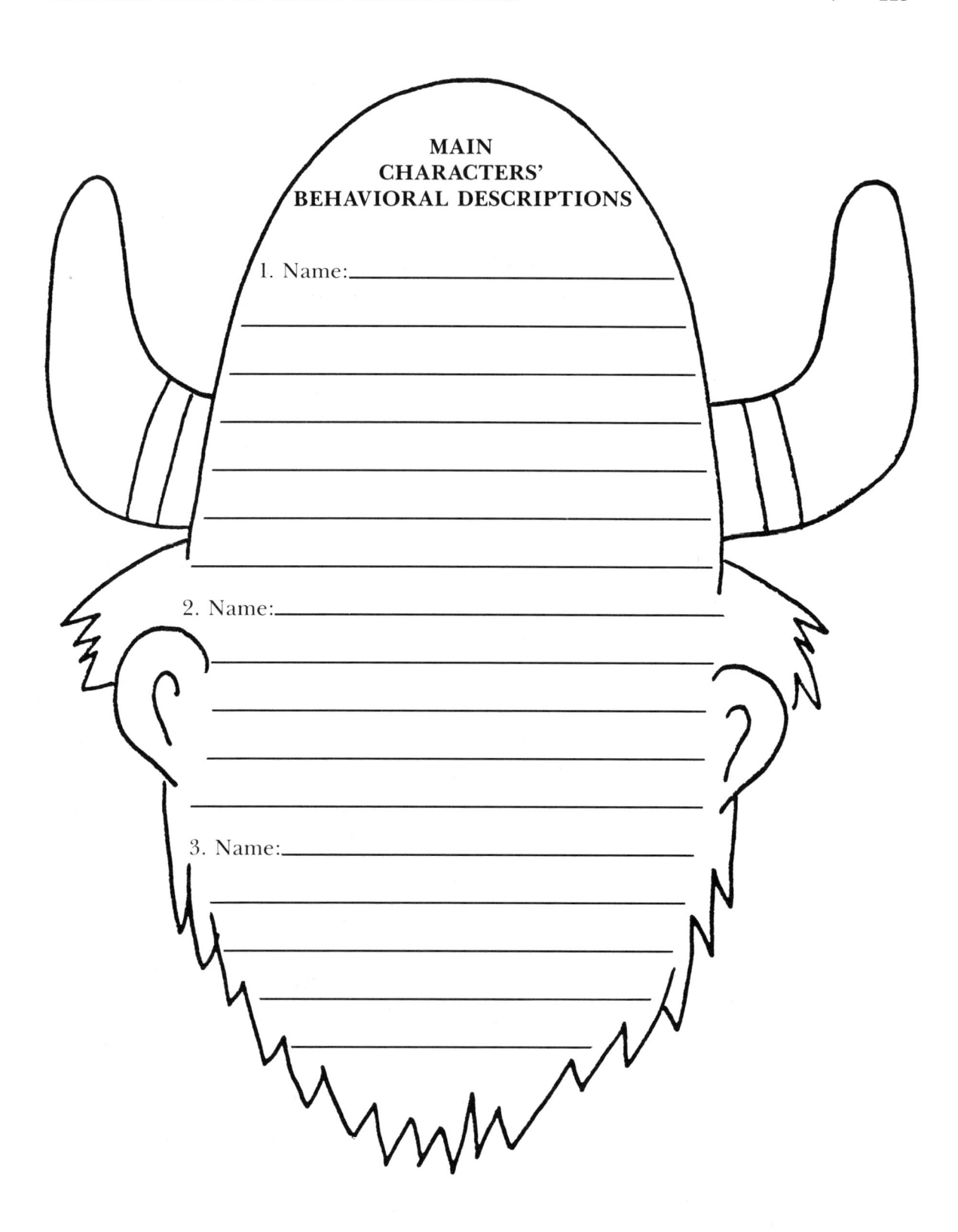

MAIN CHARACTERS' BEHAVIORAL DESCRIPTIONS

1. Name:_____
_____
_____
_____
_____
_____
_____
_____

2. Name:_____
_____
_____
_____
_____
_____

3. Name:_____
_____
_____
_____
_____
_____

Use good descriptive adjectives to describe how your main characters acted in the story, for example: cowardly, courageous, mean, considerate, mischievious, etc.

MINOR CHARACTERS V — H6

Give the names of several minor characters mentioned in your story. Write a brief description of each person.

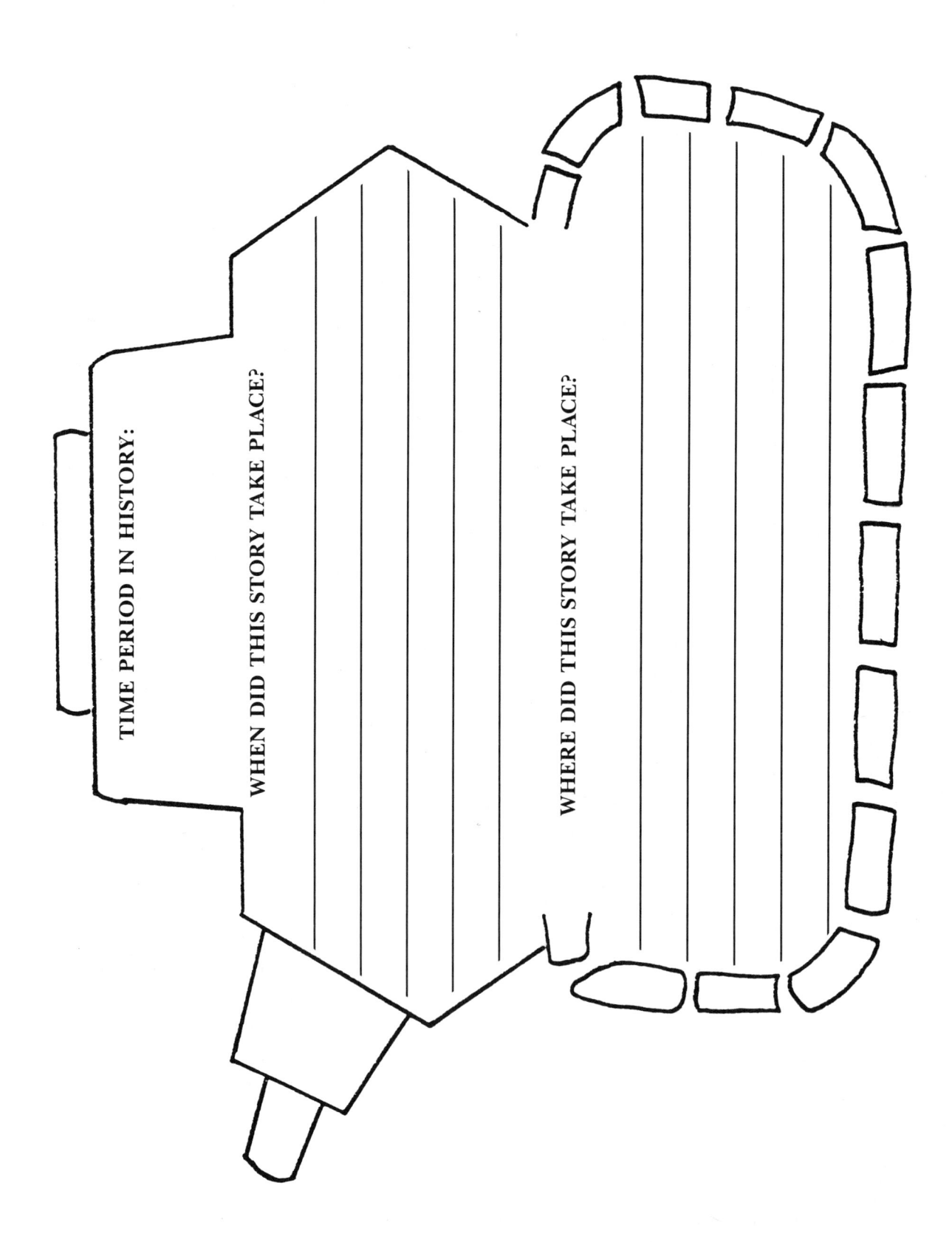

TIME PERIOD IN HISTORY V — H7

TIME PERIOD IN HISTORY:

WHEN DID THIS STORY TAKE PLACE?

WHERE DID THIS STORY TAKE PLACE?

TIME PERIOD IN HISTORY V — H8

TIME PERIOD IN HISTORY: INTERESTING FACTS

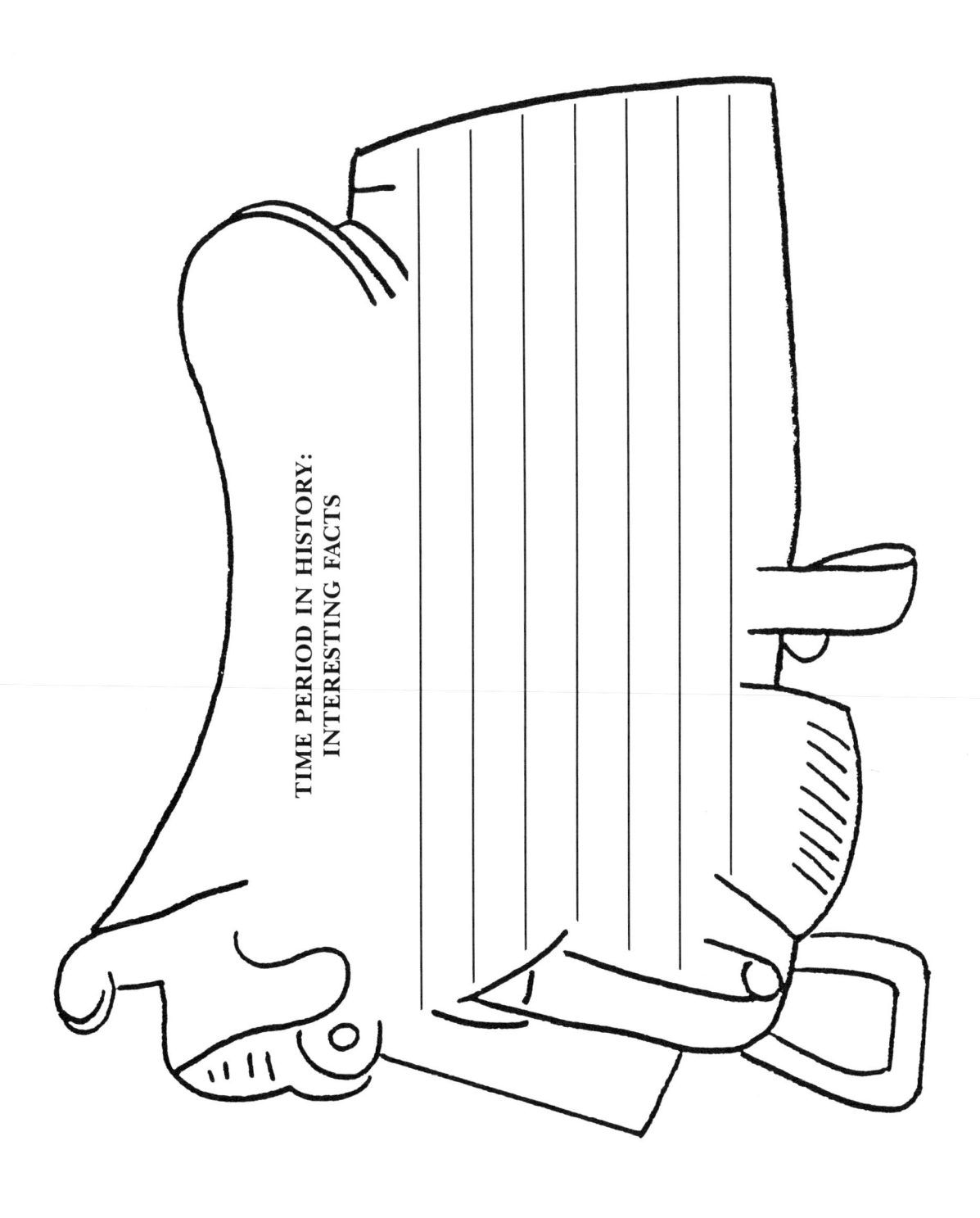

Did you learn anything else interesting about the time period in history depicted by your story that is not included on the other papers?

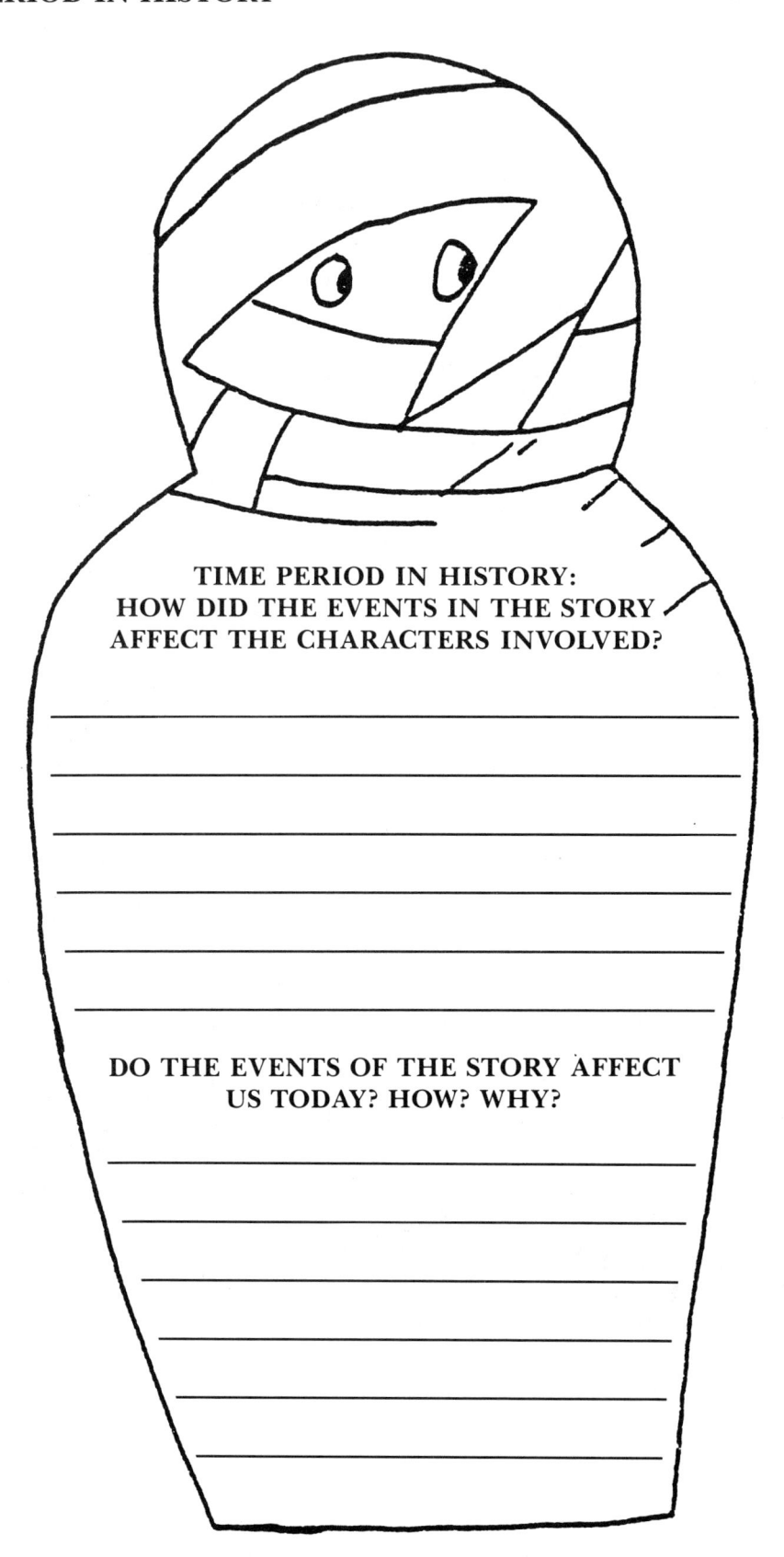

TIME PERIOD IN HISTORY V — H9

**TIME PERIOD IN HISTORY:
HOW DID THE EVENTS IN THE STORY
AFFECT THE CHARACTERS INVOLVED?**

_____
_____
_____
_____
_____
_____
_____

**DO THE EVENTS OF THE STORY AFFECT
US TODAY? HOW? WHY?**

_____
_____
_____
_____
_____
_____
_____
_____

SUPER EFFORT V — H10

SUPER EFFORT

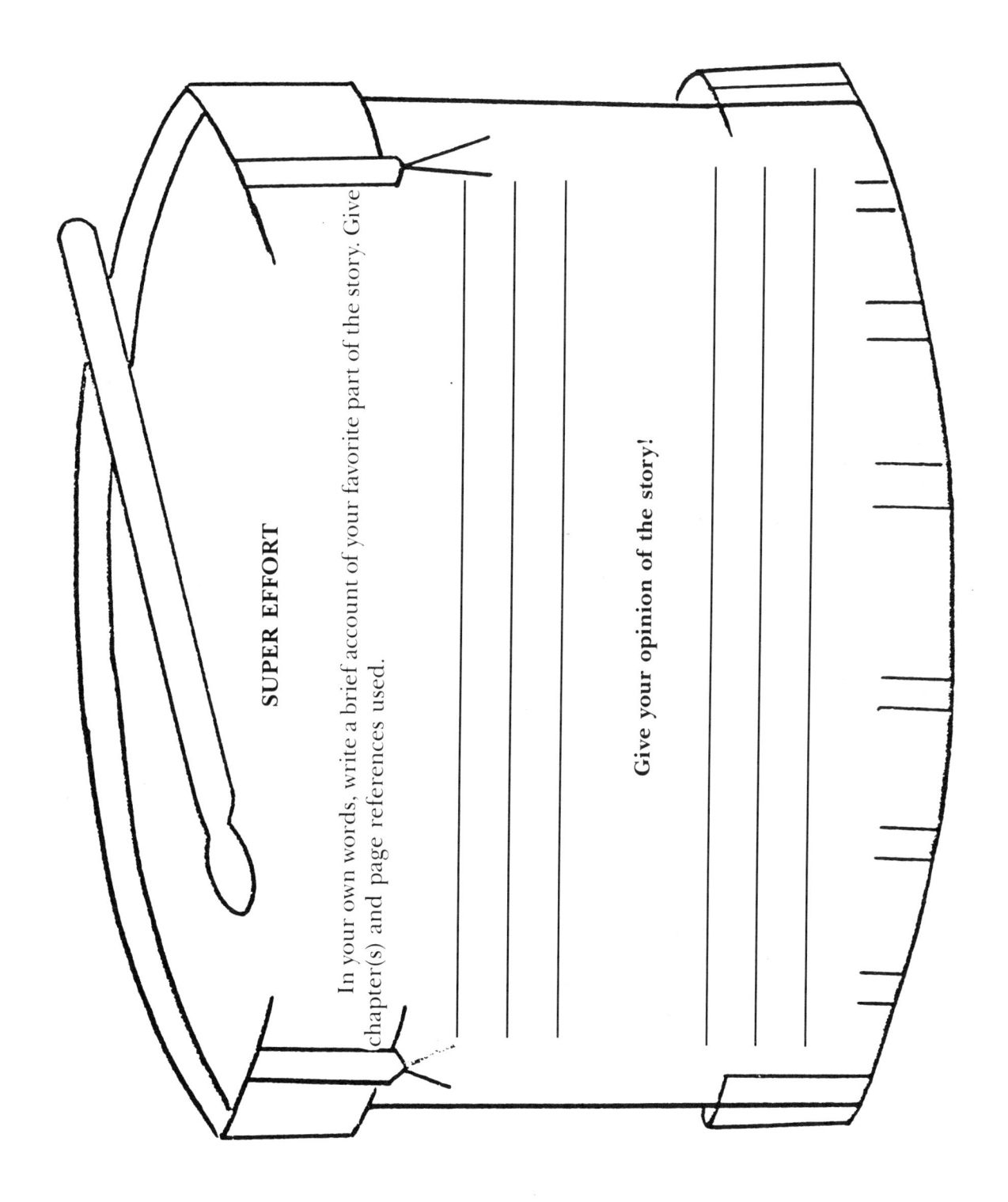

In your own words, write a brief account of your favorite part of the story. Give chapter(s) and page references used.

Give your opinion of the story!

V — M

MYSTERY STORIES

© 1983 by The Center for Applied Research in Education, Inc.

MYSTERY STORIES

V — M1

1. Choose a mystery book to read. Suggestions may be offered by your teacher or librarian. I chose _____

2. On Bibliography page V — M2, give the title of your book, the author's name, publisher, copyright date, and number of pages.

3. Study your project papers. After reading the book you have chosen, collect your information. Write the facts in NOTE FORM on outline chart V — M3.

4. When all of your information has been gathered, rewrite it on the papers provided. This time use SENTENCES. Proofread for spelling or grammar errors. Use markers, crayons, or colored pencils to color and outline the pictures.

5. If you are a good worker, try the additional page called SUPER EFFORT. Add this to your finished project.

6. Cut out the designs when completed and mount them on construction paper, make into a mobile, or use your own ideas for presentation to the class or individuals.

7. Your teacher will be glad to help you if you need any assistance.

8. APPROXIMATE TIME TO COMPLETE PROJECT: 4 — 5 hours. (This does not include the time you take to read your book.)

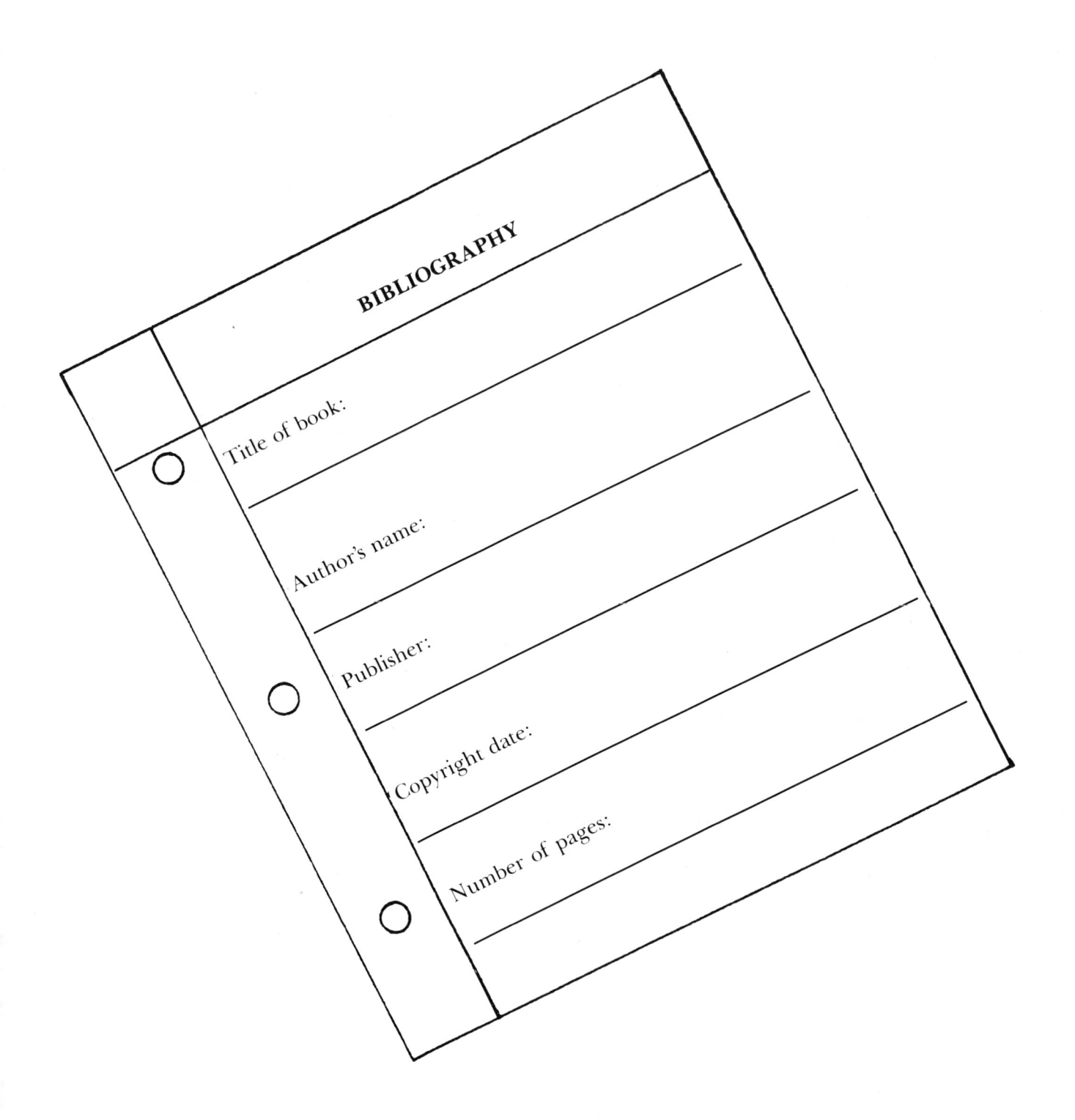

BIBLIOGRAPHY V — M2

BIBLIOGRAPHY

Title of book:

Author's name:

Publisher:

Copyright date:

Number of pages:

MYSTERY STORIES V — M3

Name_____

I chose_____   Date_____

MAIN CHARACTERS: 1._____   2._____

3._____   (No more than 3)

DESCRIPTION OF MAIN CHARACTERS

PHYSICAL DESCRIPTION	**BEHAVIORAL DESCRIPTION**
1.	1.
2.	2.
3.	3.

MINOR CHARACTERS — NAME SEVERAL AND DESCRIBE BRIEFLY

WHERE DID THE STORY TAKE PLACE?	**WHAT WAS THE MYSTERY?**	**HOW WAS IT SOLVED?**

HOW DID THE EVENTS IN THE STORY AFFECT THE CHARACTERS INVOLVED?	**INTERESTING FACTS**

DESCRIPTION OF MAIN CHARACTERS

V — M4

MAIN CHARACTERS' PHYSICAL DESCRIPTIONS

1. Name: _____
   _____
   _____
   _____
   _____

2. Name: _____
   _____
   _____
   _____
   _____
   _____

3. Name: _____
   _____
   _____
   _____

Did you tell your characters' ages and how they looked and dressed in the story you read?

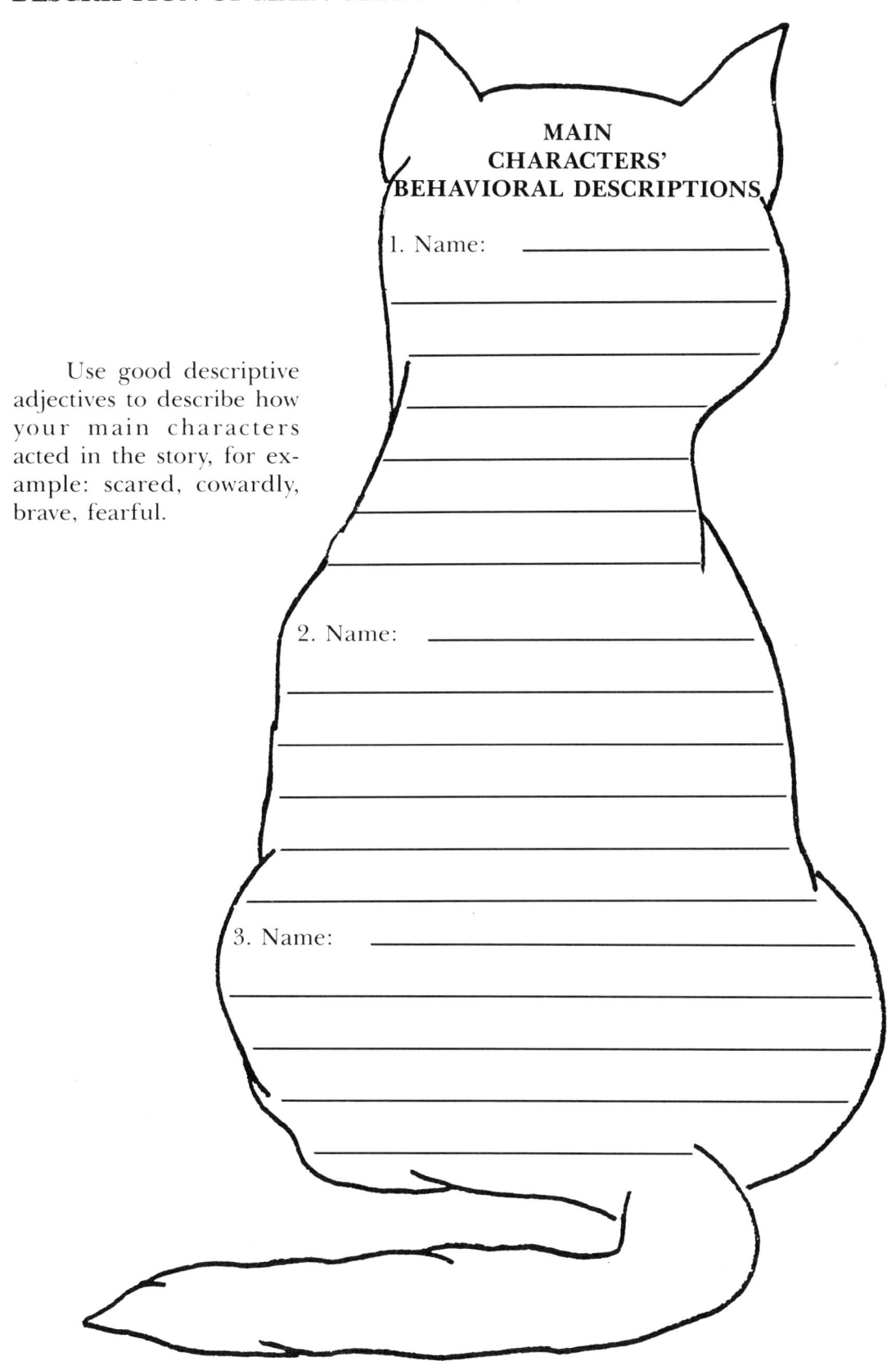

DESCRIPTION OF MAIN CHARACTERS

V — M5

MAIN CHARACTERS' BEHAVIORAL DESCRIPTIONS

1. Name: _____

Use good descriptive adjectives to describe how your main characters acted in the story, for example: scared, cowardly, brave, fearful.

2. Name: _____

3. Name: _____

MINOR CHARACTERS　　　　　　　　　　　　　　　　　　　　　　　　　　**V — M6**

MINOR CHARACTERS

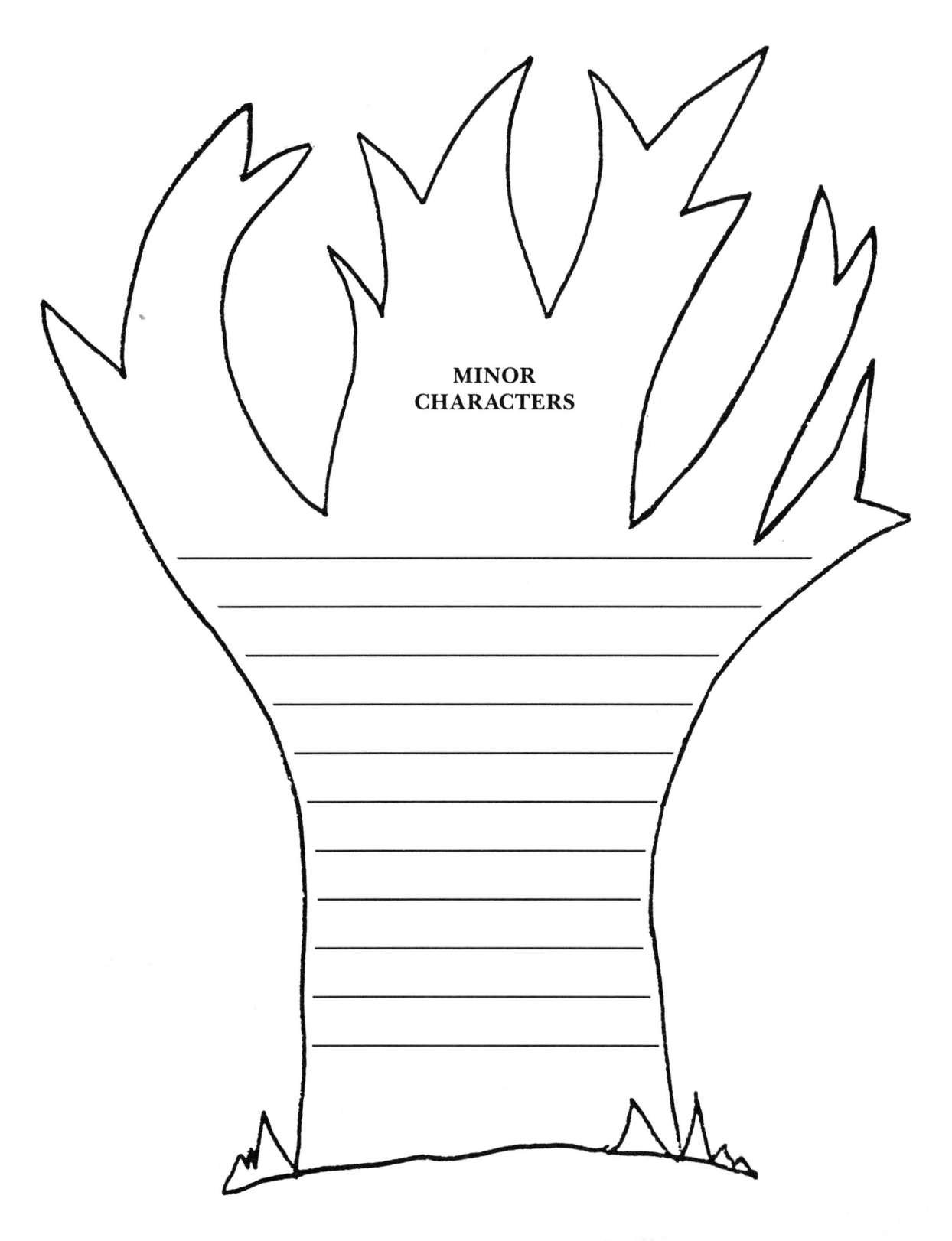

Give the names of several minor characters mentioned in your story. Write a brief description of each person.

WHERE DID THE STORY TAKE PLACE? V — M7

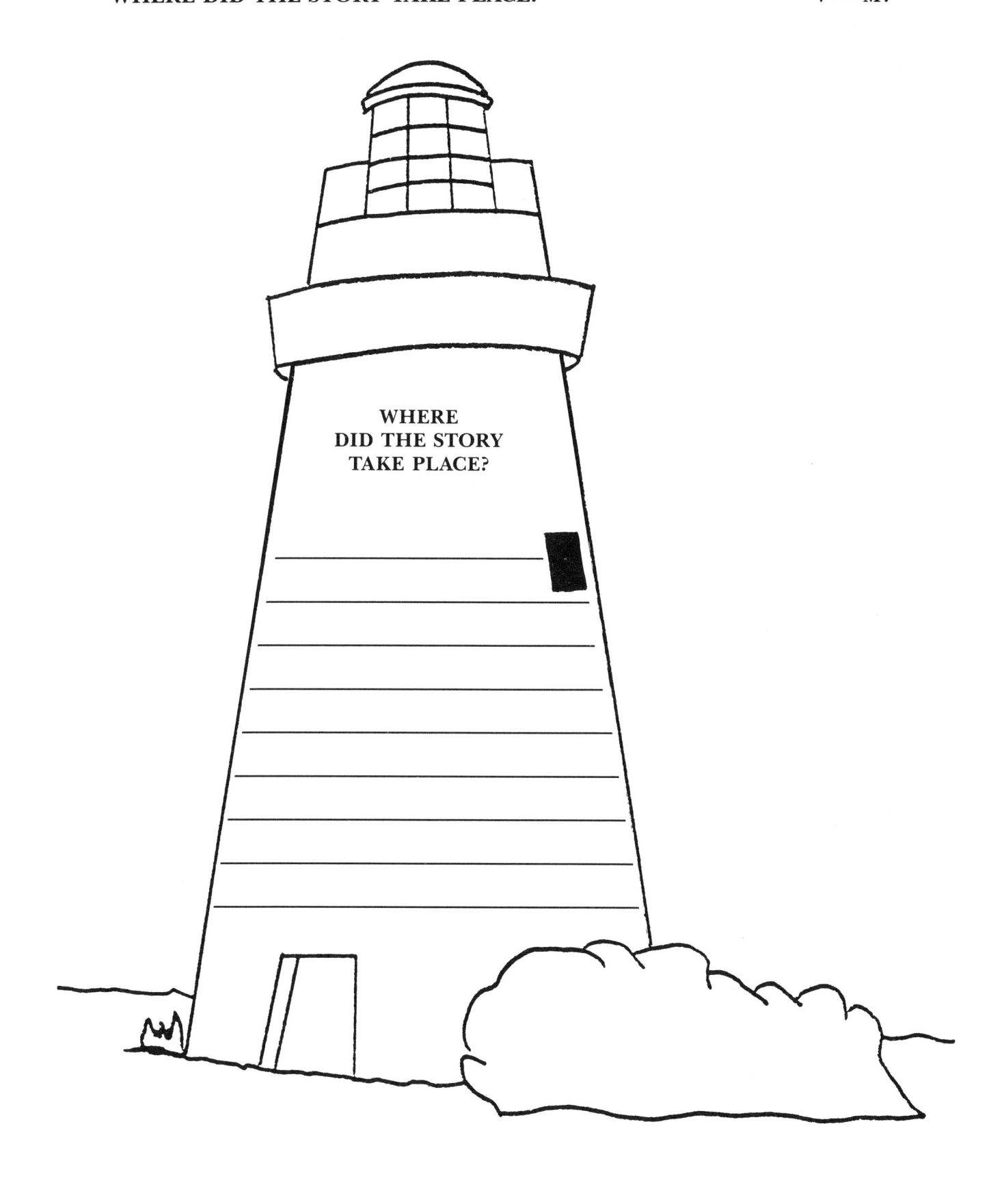

WHERE
DID THE STORY
TAKE PLACE?

_____
_____
_____
_____
_____
_____
_____
_____
_____

WHAT WAS THE MYSTERY?　　　　　　　　　　　　　　　　　　　　V — M8

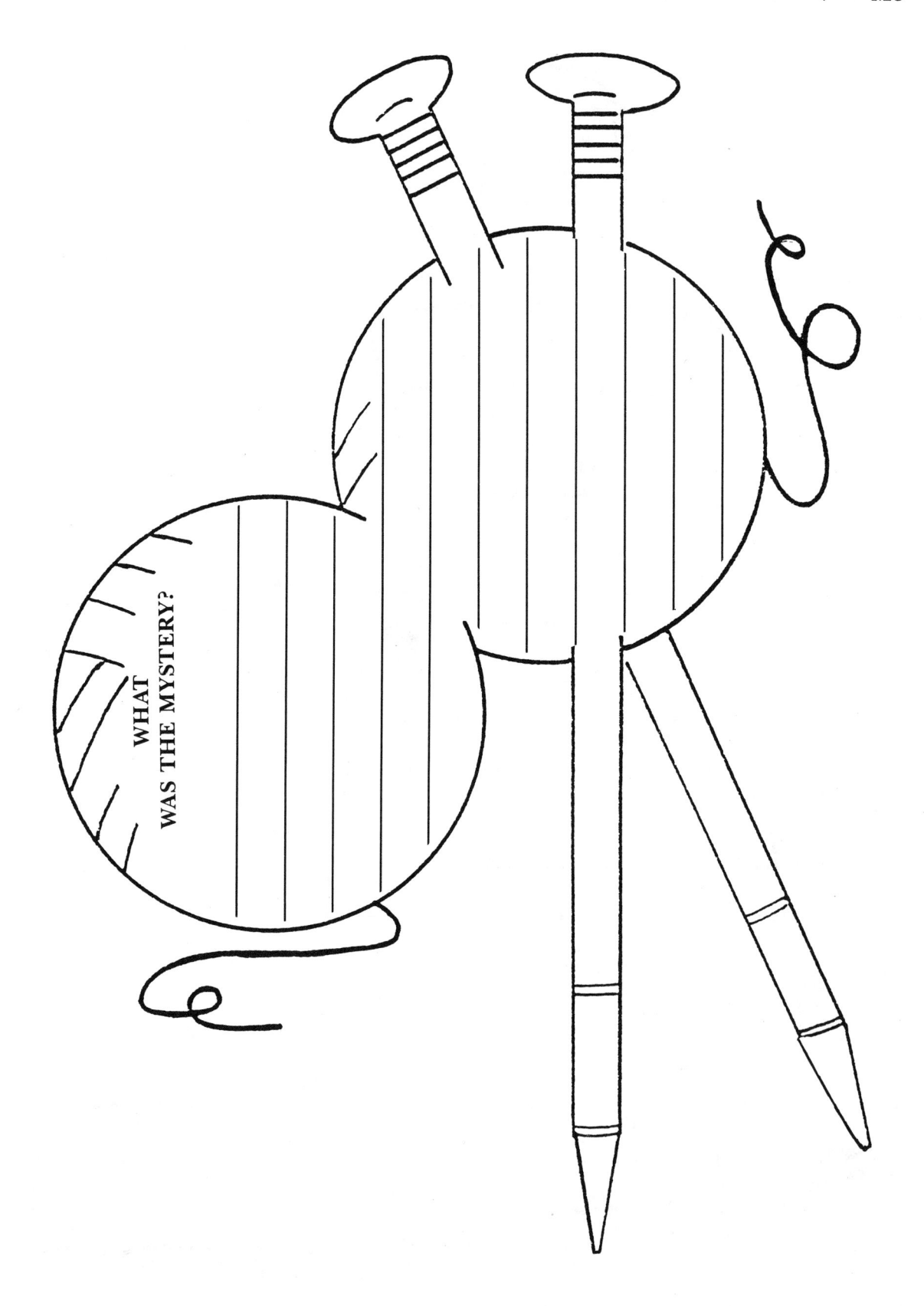

HOW WAS IT SOLVED? V — M9

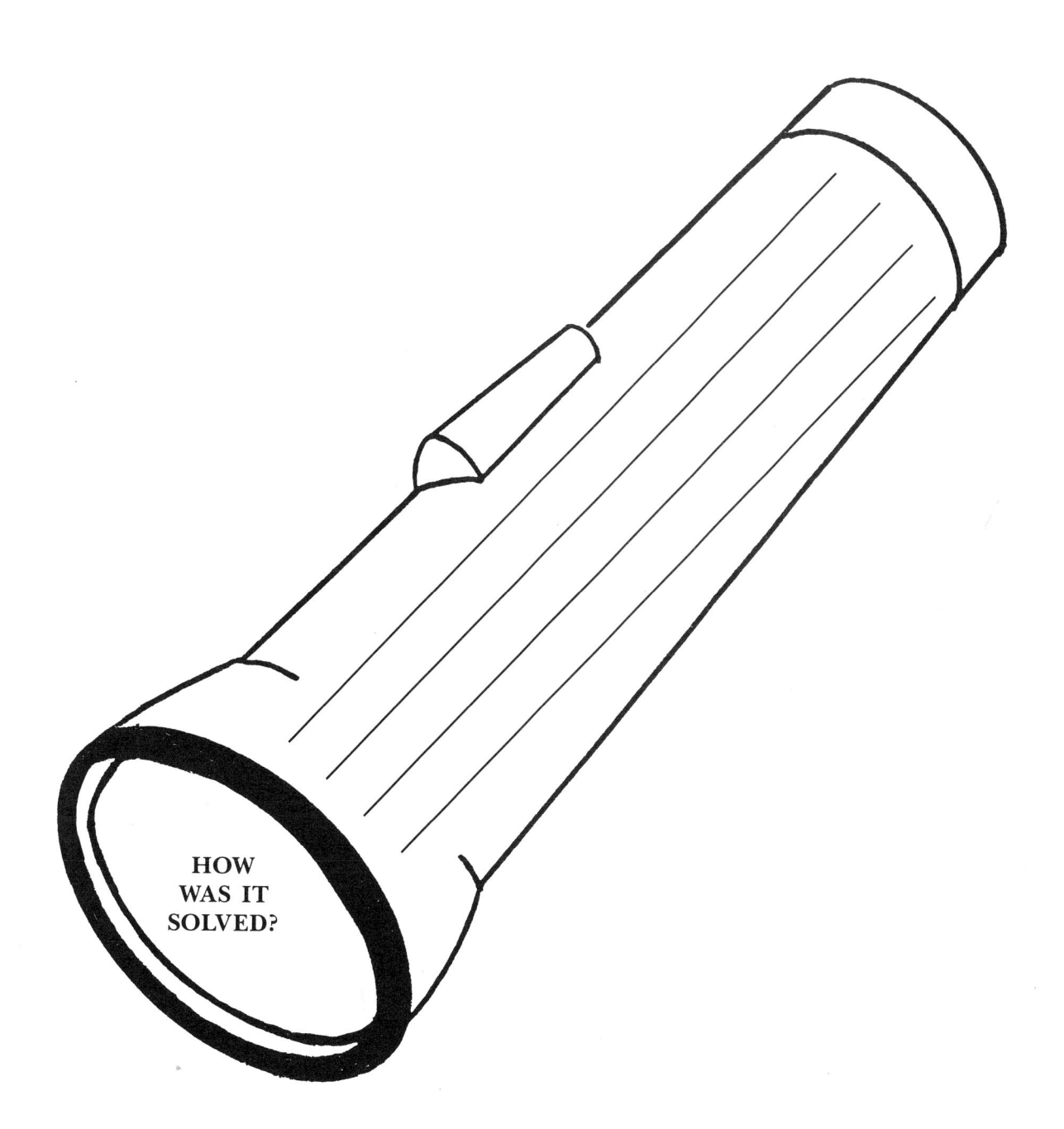

HOW WAS IT SOLVED?

**HOW DID THE EVENTS IN THE STORY
AFFECT THE CHARACTERS INVOLVED?**

**HOW DID THE EVENTS IN THE STORY
AFFECT THE CHARACTERS INVOLVED?**

_____
_____
_____
_____
_____
_____
_____
_____

INTERESTING FACTS V — M11

INTERESTING FACTS

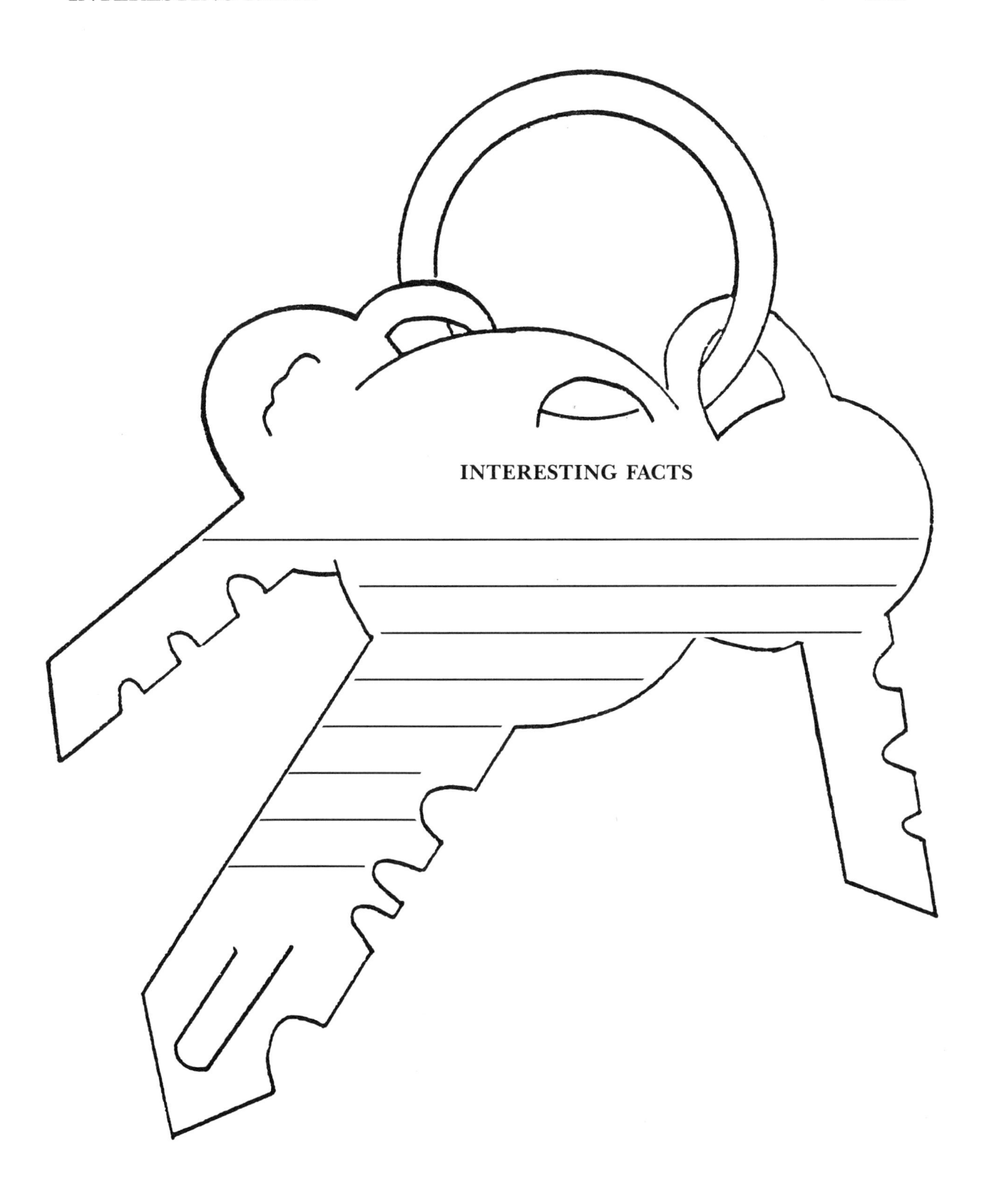

Did you learn anything else interesting from your story that is not included on the other papers?

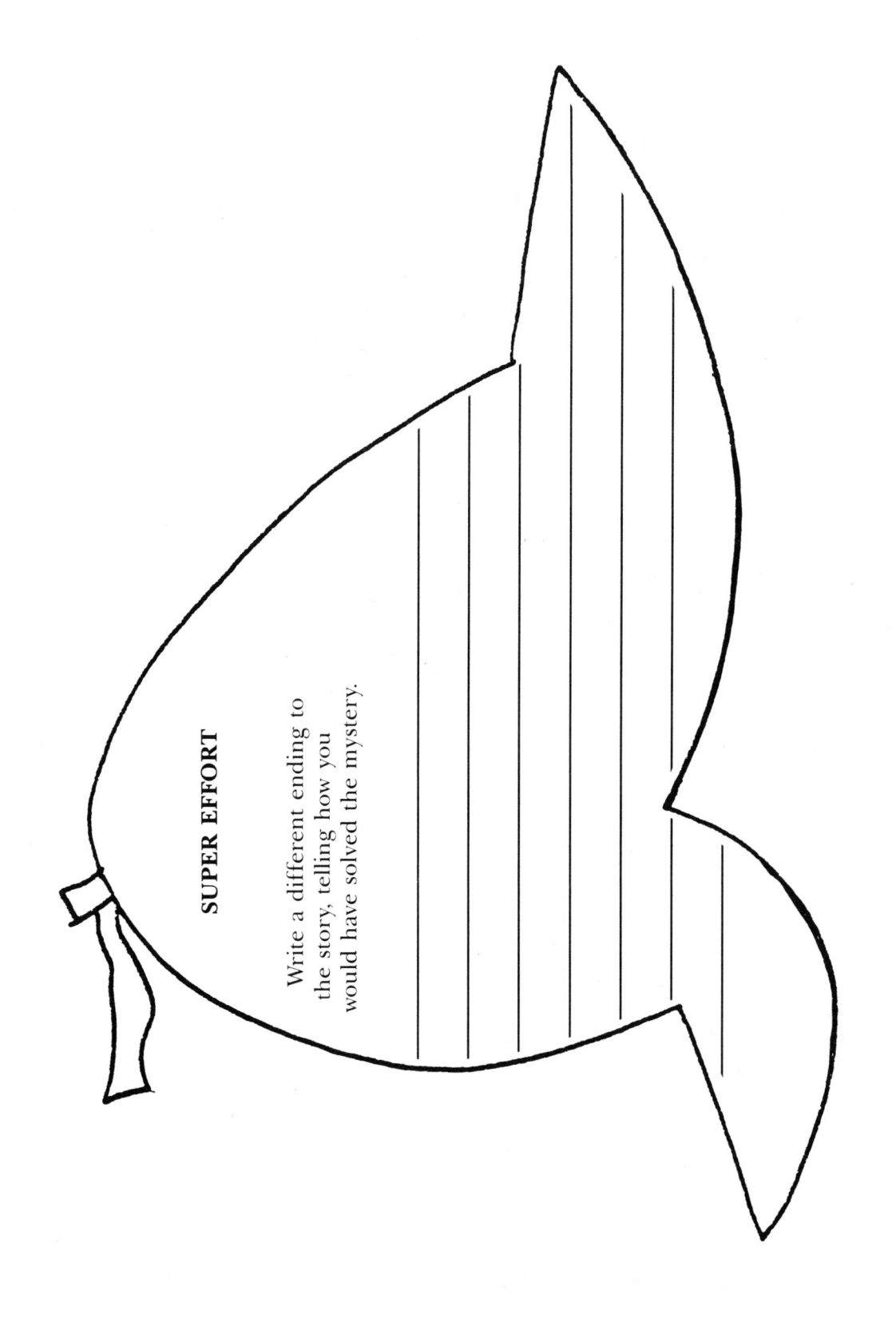

SUPER EFFORT V — M12

SUPER EFFORT

Write a different ending to the story, telling how you would have solved the mystery.

V—P

POETRY

POETRY

1. Choose *two* poetry books to read completely and several others to browse through.

2. On Bibliography page V — P2, give the title, author's name, publisher, copyright date, and number of pages for the two books you have read in full.

3. Study your project papers. After reading the books you have chosen, collect your information. Write the facts in NOTE FORM on outline chart V — P3.

4. When all of your information has been gathered, rewrite it on the papers provided. This time use SENTENCES. Proofread for spelling or grammar errors. Use markers, crayons, or colored pencils to color and outline the pictures.

5. If you are a good worker, try the additional page called SUPER EFFORT. Add this to your finished project.

6. Cut out the completed designs and mount them on construction paper, make into a mobile, or use your own ideas for presentation to the class or individuals.

7. Your teacher will be glad to help you if you need any assistance.

8. APPROXIMATE TIME TO COMPLETE PROJECT: 4 — 5 hours. (This does not include the time you take to read your books.)

BIBLIOGRAPHY   **V — P2**

BIBLIOGRAPHY

1. Title of book_____

   Author's name_____

   Publisher_____

   Copyright date_____Number of pages_____

2. Title of book_____

   Author's name_____

   Publisher_____

   Copyright date_____Number of pages_____

POETRY

V — P3

Name_____

I chose_____ Date_____

and_____

WHAT KIND OF POETRY DO YOU LIKE BEST? WHY?

WHAT KIND OF POETRY DO YOU LIKE LEAST? WHY?

EXPLAIN THE DIFFERENCE BETWEEN HUMOROUS AND SERIOUS POETRY

INTERESTING FACTS

WHAT KIND OF POETRY DO YOU LIKE BEST? WHY?

WHAT KIND OF POETRY DO YOU LIKE BEST? WHY?

_____
_____
_____
_____
_____
_____

In the space provided, draw several illustrations of what you like *best* to read about in poetry. Name your drawings.

WHAT KIND OF POETRY DO YOU LIKE LEAST? WHY? V — P5

WHAT KIND OF POETRY DO YOU LIKE LEAST? WHY?
_____
_____
_____
_____
_____
_____
_____

In the space provided, draw several illustrations of what you like *least* to read about in poetry. Name your drawings.

EXPLAIN THE DIFFERENCE BETWEEN HUMOROUS AND SERIOUS POETRY

V — P6

EXPLAIN THE DIFFERENCE BETWEEN HUMOROUS AND SERIOUS POETRY

_____
_____
_____
_____
_____
_____
_____

INTERESTING FACTS　　　　　　　　　　　　　　　　　　　　　　　　　V — P7

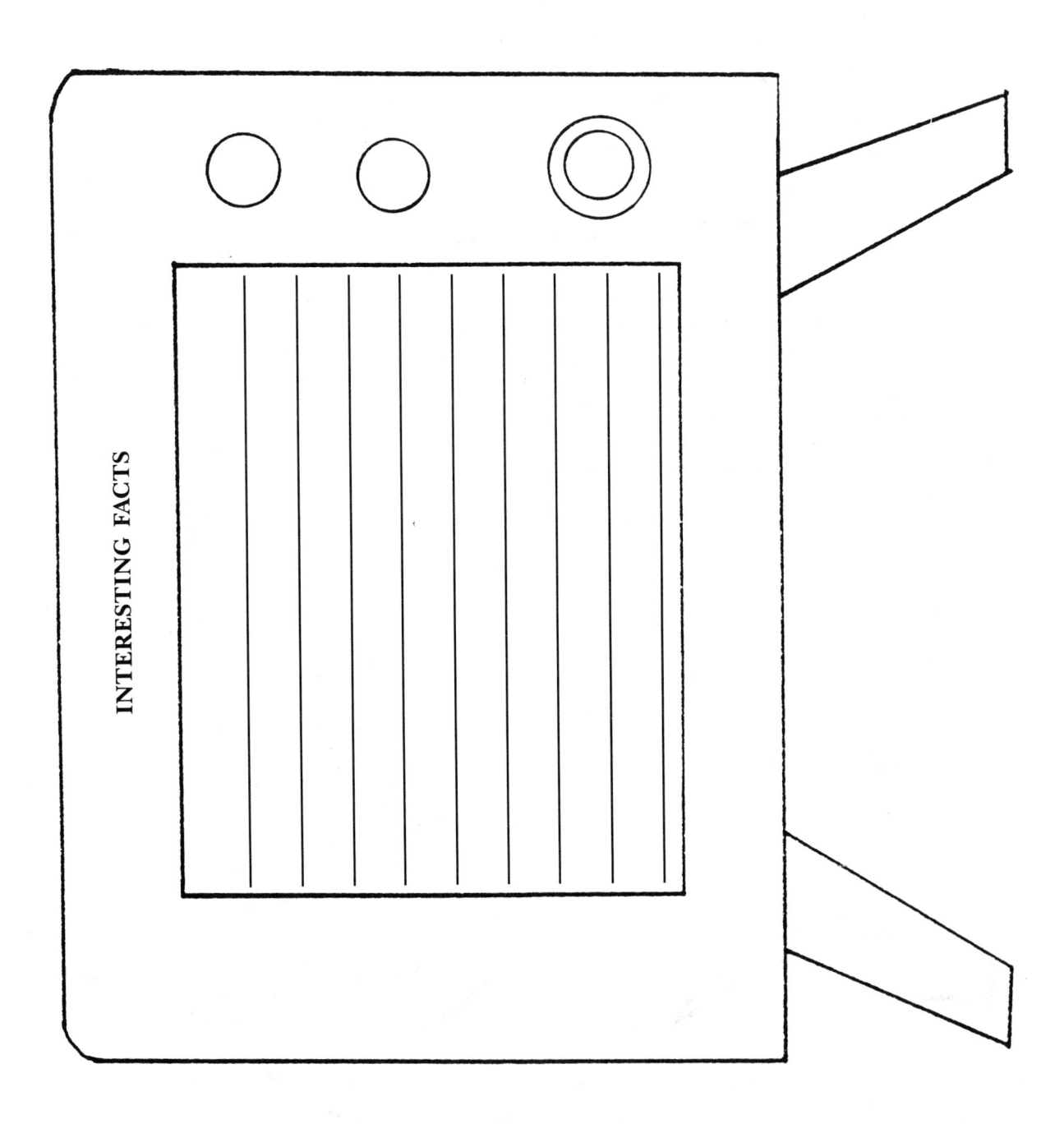

Did you learn anything else interesting about poetry while reading your books that has not been included elsewhere on your papers?

SUPER EFFORT V — P8

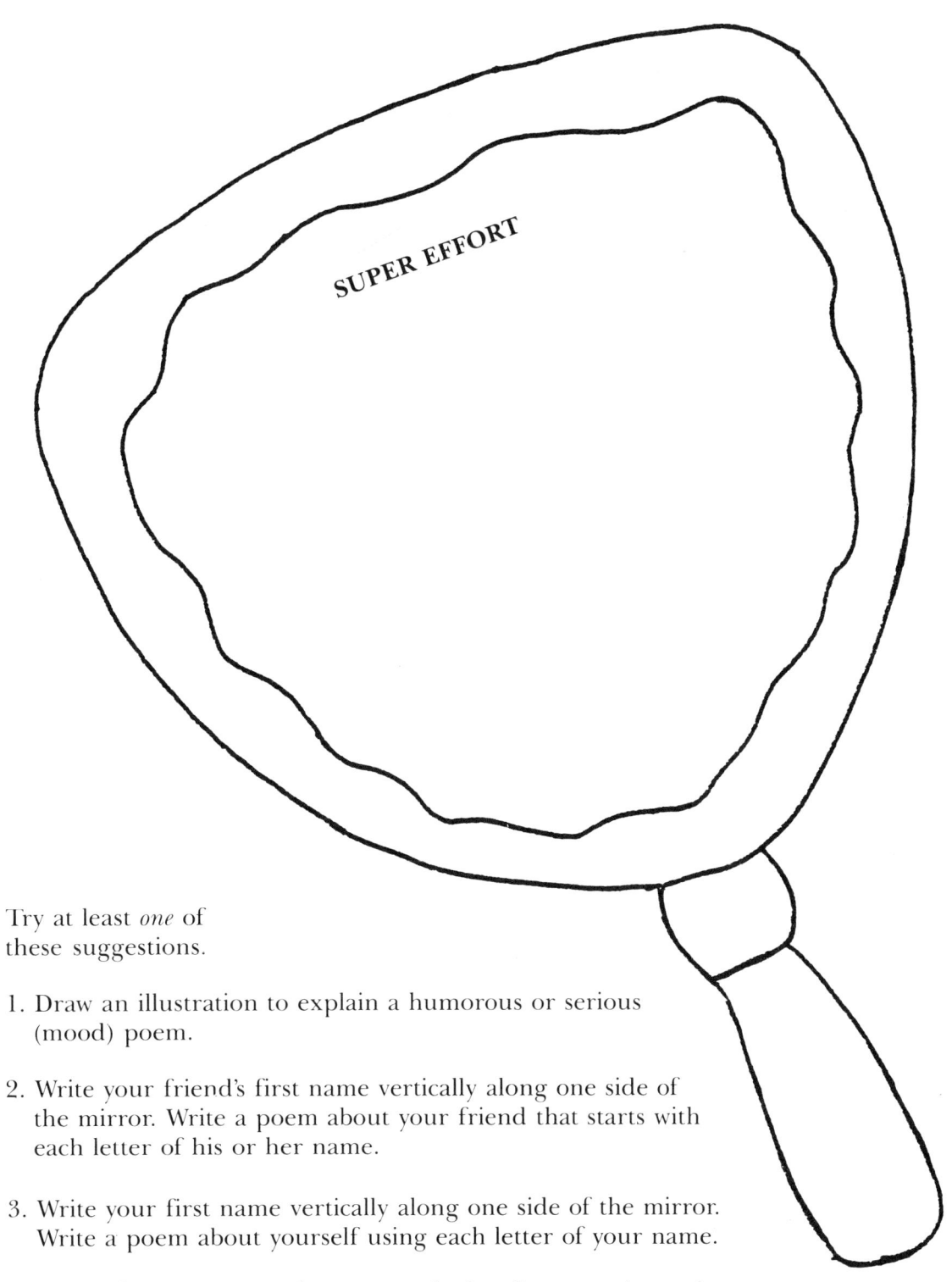

SUPER EFFORT

Try at least *one* of these suggestions.

1. Draw an illustration to explain a humorous or serious (mood) poem.

2. Write your friend's first name vertically along one side of the mirror. Write a poem about your friend that starts with each letter of his or her name.

3. Write your first name vertically along one side of the mirror. Write a poem about yourself using each letter of your name.

4. Poets often use expressions or words that fit categories such as feelings, hearing, tasting, seeing, and smelling. Find an example for several or all and write them in your mirror.

V — S

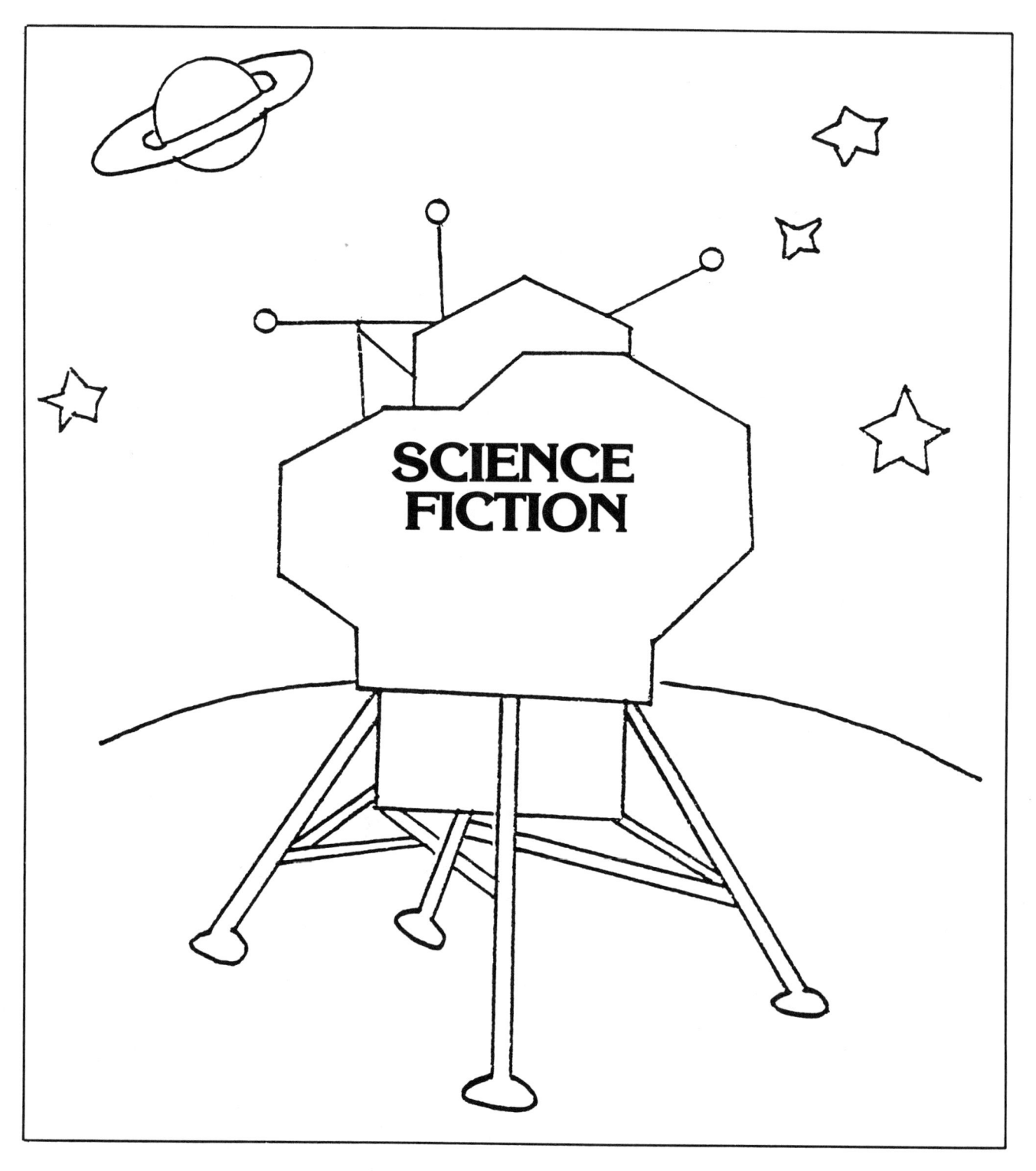

SCIENCE FICTION V — S1

1. Choose a science fiction book to read. Suggestions may be offered by your teacher or librarian. I chose _____

2. On Bibliography page V — S2 give the title of your book, the author's name, publisher, copyright date, and number of pages.

3. Study your project papers. After reading the book you have chosen, collect your information. Write the facts in NOTE FORM on outline chart V — S3.

4. When all of your information has been gathered, rewrite it on the papers provided. This time use SENTENCES. Proofread for spelling or grammar errors. Use markers, crayons, or colored pencils to color and outline the pictures.

5. If you are a good worker, try the additional page called SUPER EFFORT. Add this to your finished project.

6. Cut out the designs when completed and mount them on construction paper, make into a mobile, or use your own ideas for presentation to the class or individuals.

7. Your teacher will be glad to help you if you need any assistance.

8. APPROXIMATE TIME TO COMPLETE PROJECT: 4 — 5 hours. (This does not include the time you take to read your book.)

BIBLIOGRAPHY

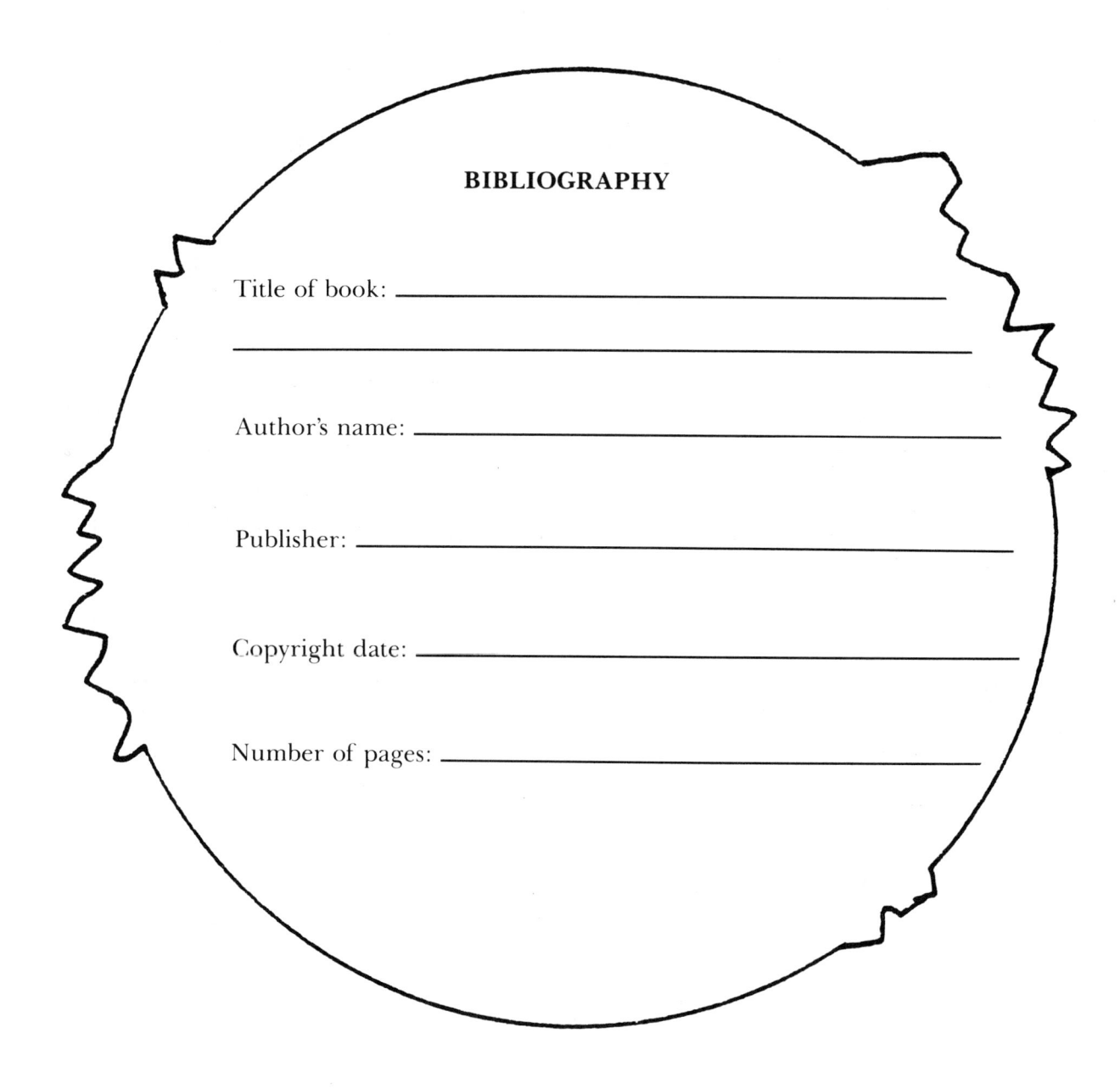

BIBLIOGRAPHY

Title of book: _____

_____

Author's name: _____

Publisher: _____

Copyright date: _____

Number of pages: _____

SCIENCE FICTION   V — S3

Name _____

I chose _____   Date _____

MAIN CHARACTERS: 1. _____   2. _____

                         3. _____   (No more than 3)

DESCRIPTION OF MAIN CHARACTERS

PHYSICAL DESCRIPTION	**BEHAVIORAL DESCRIPTION**
1.	1.
2.	2.
3.	3.

MINOR CHARACTERS — NAME SEVERAL AND DESCRIBE BRIEFLY

WHERE DID THE STORY TAKE PLACE?	**WHAT WAS THE MAIN PLOT OF THE STORY?**	**HOW DID THE STORY END?**

INTERESTING FACTS

DESCRIPTION OF MAIN CHARACTERS

V — S4

MAIN CHARACTERS' PHYSICAL DESCRIPTIONS

1. Name: _____

   _____
   _____
   _____

2. Name: _____

   _____
   _____
   _____

3. Name: _____

   _____
   _____
   _____
   _____

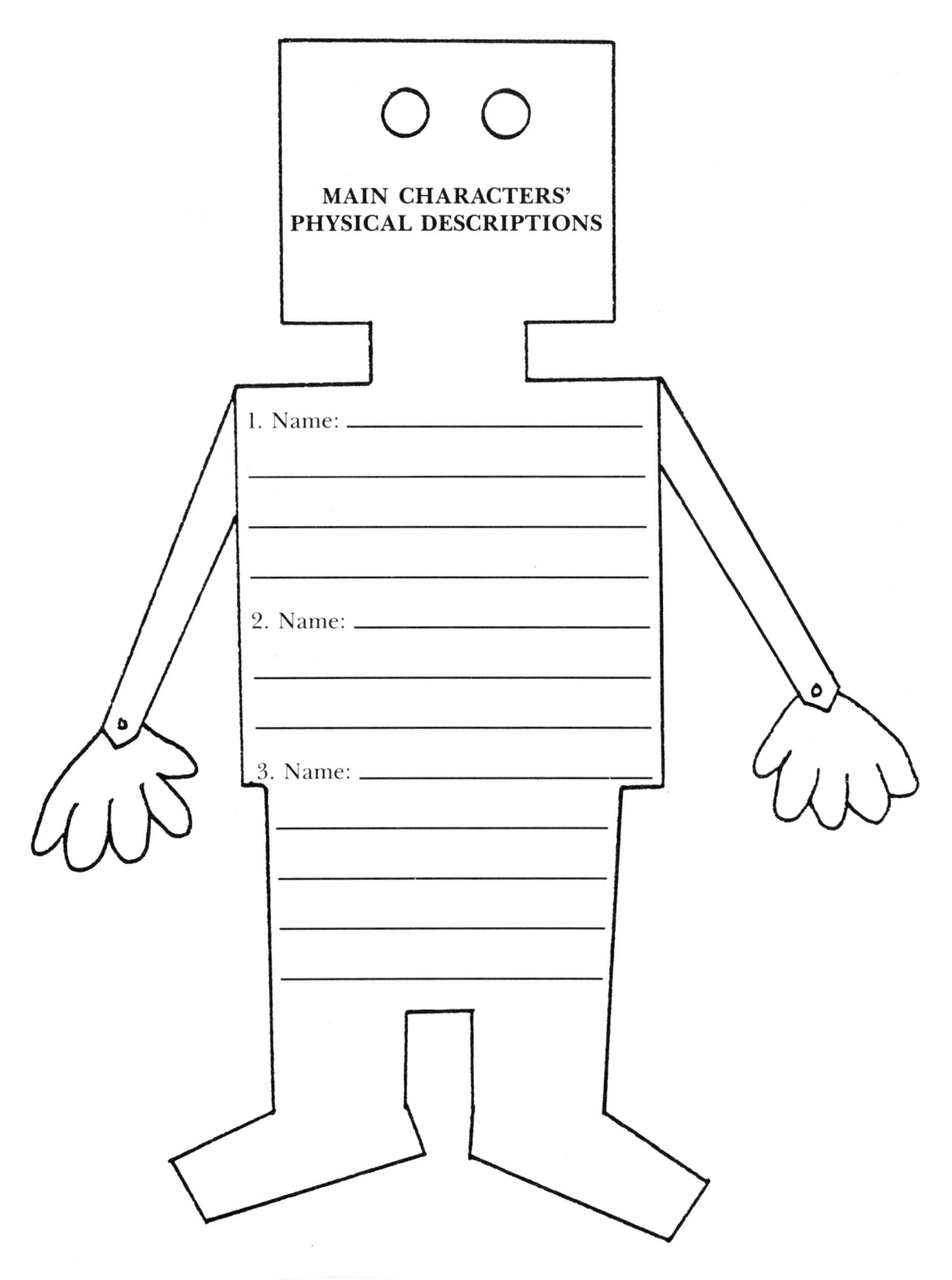

Use good descriptive adjectives to describe how your main characters acted in the story, for example, cowardly, courageous, mean, considerate, etc.

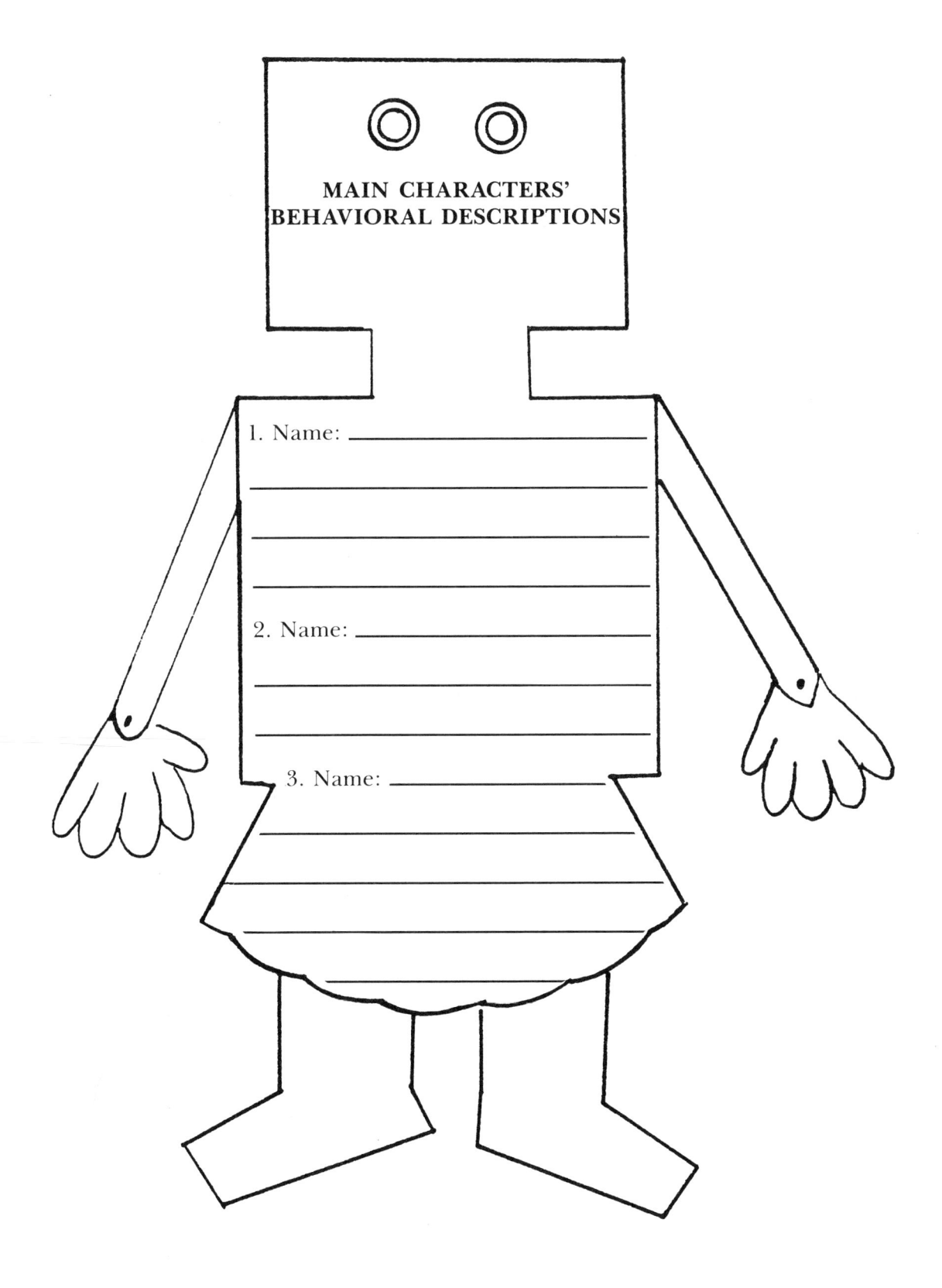

DESCRIPTION OF MAIN CHARACTERS V — S5

MAIN CHARACTERS' BEHAVIORAL DESCRIPTIONS

1. Name: _____

2. Name: _____

3. Name: _____

MINOR CHARACTERS V — S6

MINOR CHARACTERS

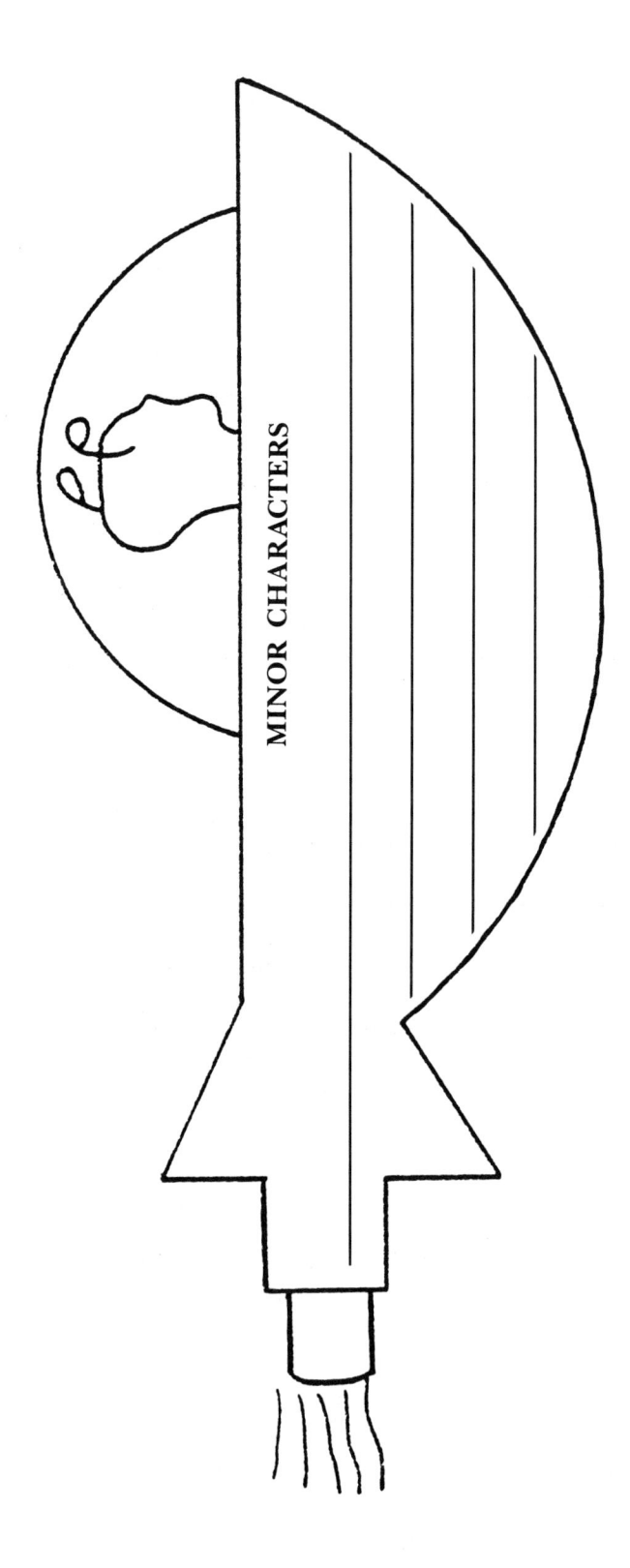

Give the names of several minor characters mentioned in your story. Write a brief description of each character.

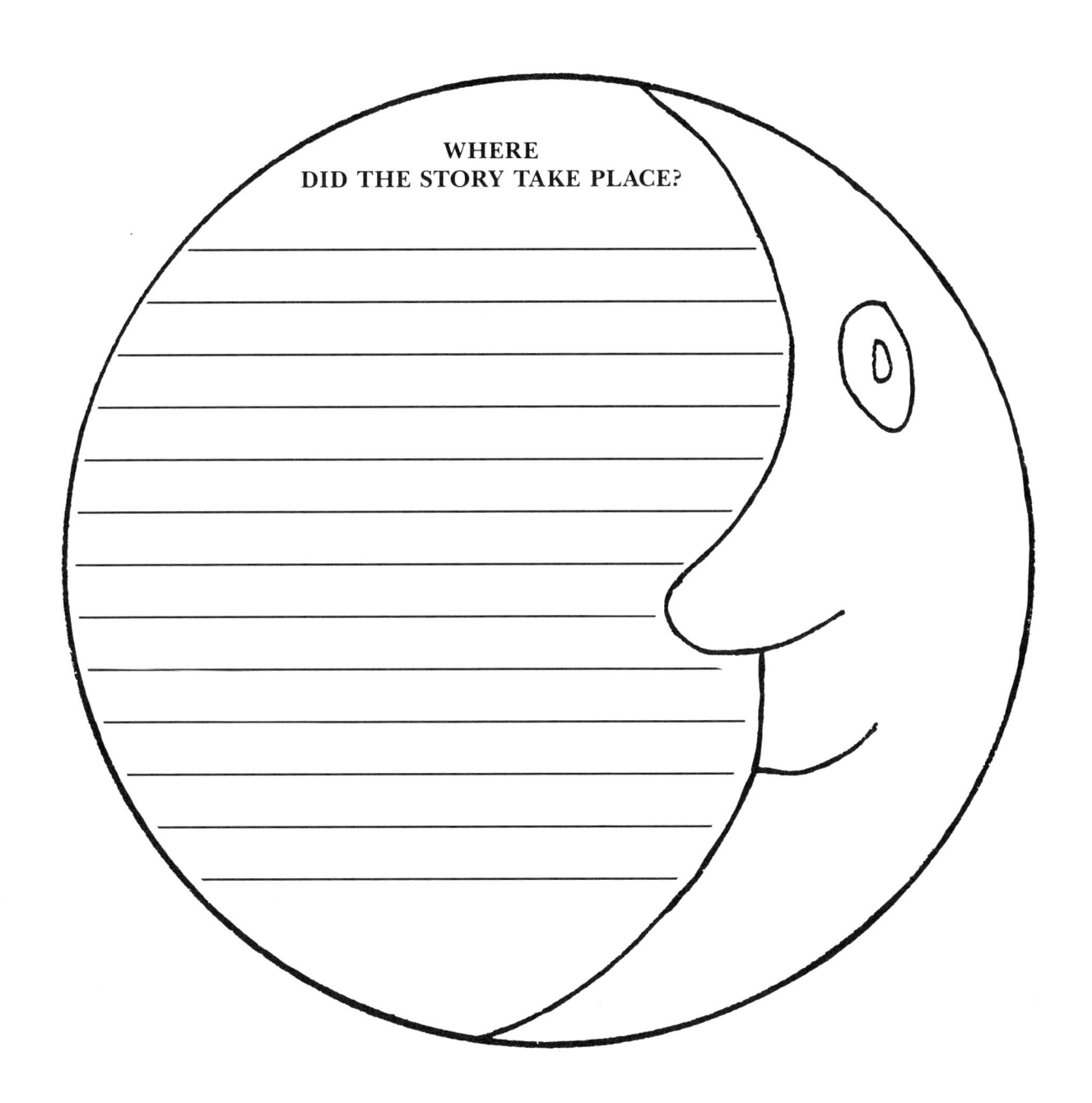

WHERE DID THE STORY TAKE PLACE? V — S7

WHERE DID THE STORY TAKE PLACE?

_____
_____
_____
_____
_____
_____
_____
_____
_____
_____
_____
_____

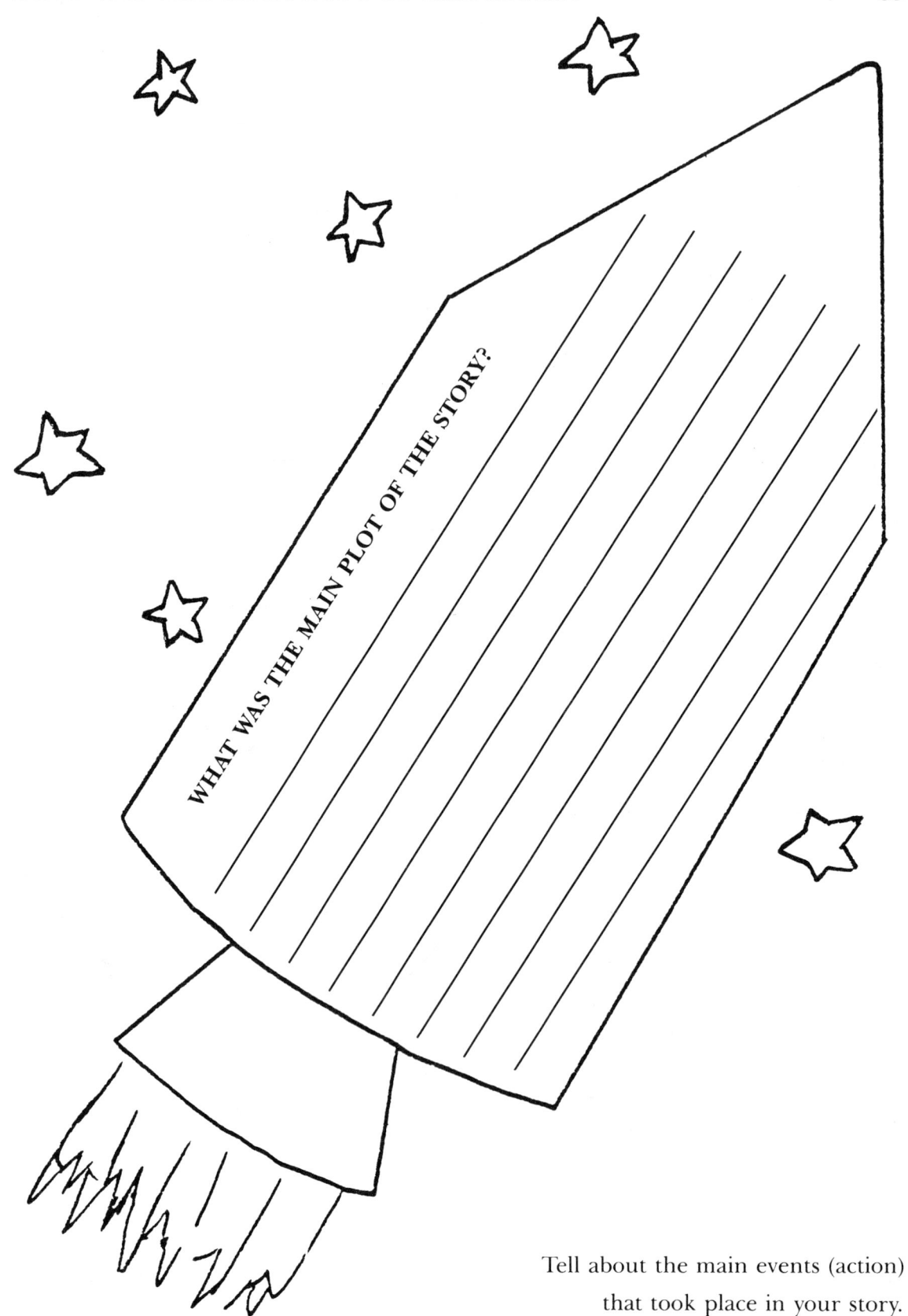

WHAT WAS THE MAIN PLOT OF THE STORY? V — S8

WHAT WAS THE MAIN PLOT OF THE STORY?

Tell about the main events (action) that took place in your story.

HOW DID THE STORY END? V — S9

?

HOW
DID THE STORY
END?

_____
_____
_____
_____
_____
_____
_____
_____

INTERESTING FACTS V — S10

INTERESTING FACTS